THE
FIVE PRINCIPLES
GLOBAL *of*
LEADERSHIP

How To Manage the Complexities of Global Leadership

Jay Clark, Ph.D.

WESTBOW
PRESS
A DIVISION OF THOMAS NELSON
& ZONDERVAN

Scripture quotations are from The Holy Bible, English Standard Version® (ESV®), copyright © 2001 by Crossway, a publishing ministry of Good News Publishers. Used by permission. All rights reserved.

This book is a work of non-fiction. Unless otherwise noted, the author and the publisher make no explicit guarantees as to the accuracy of the information contained in this book and in some cases, names of people and places have been altered to protect their privacy.

WestBow Press books may be ordered through booksellers or by contacting:

WestBow Press
A Division of Thomas Nelson & Zondervan
1663 Liberty Drive
Bloomington, IN 47403
www.westbowpress.com
1 (866) 928-1240

ISBN: 978-1-4908-8301-4 (sc)
ISBN: 978-1-4908-8302-1 (hc)
ISBN: 978-1-4908-8300-7 (e)

Library of Congress Control Number: 2015909004

Print information available on the last page.

WestBow Press rev. date: 06/11/2015

Contents

Acknowledgements

The more I travel around the world, the more heroes I meet. The global leader today is challenged in many different ways and to have the courage to overcome these challenges is an impressive trait. I thank all the global leaders I've written about in this book and the many others I've served. I am honored to know you and serve with you in making a global impact.

I would also like to thank Gwen Ash and the team at Westbow Publishing who have been extremely patient with me entering the world of book publishing.

My family also deserves my gratitude for helping me write this book. My dad and mom, Billy and Linda Clark, provided support and encouragement and also looked over the manuscripts for those hard-to-find mistakes. The encouragement of my brother, John Clark, helped make this book a reality. I thank my daughters Sarah Grace, Hannah, Rebekah, Deborah, and Leah for their sacrifices that allowed me to finish the book.

Finally, I would like to thank my beloved. My wife has not only made me a better person but also made me a better writer and thinker. Thanks sweetheart for the hours of work on this book.

PART 1

*Background of
Global Leadership*

1

Why Global Leadership?

I was introduced to globalization in the summer of 1998 when I went overseas for an MBA study abroad program. It was my first trip outside of North America, and although I was fascinated by the beauty of Prague, what intrigued me most was the complexity of doing business in another culture. The challenge of researching a market progressing from communism to capitalism was captivating and not the ordinary business environment I had experienced the previous three years working in U.S. financial services.

In 2000, I added to my global leadership experience by starting a training division for the company I worked for in Amman, Jordan. Being a young, arrogant MBA graduate, I felt completely qualified to start the business and thought such a small country offered minimal complexities. I was terribly wrong. It actually proved more complex due to the political environment, religious differences, learning differences, and the industry itself. The training I had performed for small and medium-sized American manufacturers during my graduate research assistantship was not sufficient experience to promote me to expert trainer in Jordan. It was a great lesson to learn at an early age.

I progressed as a global leader in 2007 when I founded a consulting company in Hong Kong. Not only did I start the company, but my family (my wife and two children at that time) moved with me to Hong Kong. Focusing on the emerging market in China and Southeast Asia was challenging and exhilarating. We were able to work with great companies in China for seven years, but in the end the venture could not be sustained. The failure wasn't due to lack of effort or ability but a series of events including the Sichuan Earthquake and the Global Crisis. My company, with offices in Dallas and Hong Kong, did not have the funding necessary to take these hits, so it began a slow decline finally ending with the company closing in 2013.

I started academically studying leadership, specifically global leadership, in 2011 when I entered a Ph.D. program. Academia by nature is full of theories, and the theories do not always align with real experiences. But the world of leadership studies was fresh and inspiring, and I started blurring the lines between research and practice in the leadership field. As I synthesized these two areas, it brought a deeper conviction to my journey of developing global leaders.

Living in and traveling to multiple countries around the world for 15 years serving for-profit and not-for-profit organizations and spending four years researching leadership on a doctoral level has led me to write this book that synthesizes my academic research with my practical experience. The type of global leadership described in the five principles of this book is effective in any organization. The context changes, but how you manage the context and complexities will determine the effectiveness of your leadership. Working with global organizations, I see many obstacles to being a successful global leader, such as organizational development, strategic planning, and effective communication. Most leaders I work with can manage and follow a task or directive, but few can create processes such as strategic plans in which they identify local challenges and create global opportunities. Why do many leaders have difficulty developing into global leaders? The issue is based in complexity.

What makes global leadership so complex? Is it the well-known difficulties of cross-cultural communication or the inability to develop a global mindset? Although the answer is yes to both questions, they are not the main reasons. The complexity of global leadership is the most obvious when leaders have to make strategic decisions for an organization filled with crisis, conflict, and a diverse background of followers.

I was blessed to attend very good universities, study in foreign countries, and attain both a master's and a Ph.D. degree. I have traveled to and worked in over 20 countries on four continents. I have lived in small cities, large cities, international cities, and poor cities - under democracy, authoritarian rule, communism, and a mixture of both. These experiences have led me to my purpose in life. I have a passion for developing global leaders because I see a correlation between effective global leadership and building a better world.

Therefore, in the pages that follow, I provide a foundation for anyone already in global leadership, for anyone wanting to become a global leader, and for followers of global leaders. My reason for writing is not just to help global leaders but also to impact the world. Leaders are world changers, and the more responsible, effective global leaders we develop, the better the world will be.

Global Leadership and The Five Leadership Principles

By presenting the five principles of leadership in a global context, I look at the comparison of global and domestic leadership, cognitive complexity, and the development of global leaders. The first task in understanding the impact of the five principles is to form a true definition of global leadership. The definition encompasses more than just selling products across national boundaries.

A Global Leader is a person who leads across cultures with systems, processes, and relationships in a complex environment.

Complex, cross-cultural leadership can happen within the geographical boundaries of one nation or can span over oceans and across multiple countries. During my most recent trip to India, I was in a meeting with the top leaders of an organization. I noticed that the leaders segmented and formed groups that were discussing issues in their respective mother tongues. Among the 15 participants in the training, there were five different languages, five different people groups, and five different cultures. This is why English is the organizational language for most Indian companies. Even though the organization only operates inside the geographical boundaries of India, these leaders are global leaders.

Using the above definition, academic research, and my experiences, I will describe the five leadership principles that allow global leaders to manage the complexities with systems, processes, and relationships. These are the foundational principles that all leaders need to exhibit, and they are the building blocks for other necessary characteristics of an effective leader. We all have an opportunity to lead in some part of life, but those who implement principles of integrity, purpose, sacrifice, discipline, and compassion are most likely remembered as leaders who made a positive impact in their organization, communities, and world. If a person applies these characteristics to life, he or she will see fruit from the investment and build credibility and experiences that will attract followers, which is important because you are not a leader unless you have followers.

Principle #1 Integrity

Adheres to and acts in alignment with a set of core values and beliefs; keeps his/her word and commitments; establishes credibility with others by 'walking the talk'; provides honest feedback in an appropriate and helpful manner; admits mistakes; doesn't misrepresent self for personal gain; maintains confidentiality; is seen as a truthful and trustworthy leader.

In global leadership, your character is tested on a regular basis. Each crisis of leadership requires a global leader to decipher core values from cultural values. Before you can decipher these differences, you must have a clear understanding of your own core values.

Principle #2 Purpose

Understands and clearly articulates an inspired vision of the company's goals and mission; aligns team's goals with company's goals; committed to the company's core values and culture.

When leading across cultures, the global leader must carefully communicate the vision in order to ensure it is effective in reaching the target audience. Articulating a vision depends not just on the words used but on the leader's character and integrity.

Principle #3 Sacrifice

A leader is willing to sacrifice in three primary areas.

1. *Individual- Being a leader means you sacrifice individually for your purpose to be achieved.*
2. *Family- In leadership you constantly have to ask your family to sacrifice, so they must believe in your cause just as much as you do.*
3. *Those you serve- Everyone wants a piece of your attention and time. Even the people you serve will need to sacrifice and allow you to grow as a leader.*

The demands of travel alone are enough to challenge the sacrificial ability of a global leader and his or her family. But an even greater challenge for a global leader is sacrificing one's local identity in order to gain global followers.

Principle #4 Discipline

Discipline is an aspect of self-control. A leader has to be disciplined in many areas, but the two most important are time and priorities. The leader who is disciplined with time and priorities accomplishes goals and objectives.

Virtual teams and time zone differences are some of the challenges that require the global leader to manage time and priorities well. The ability to lead change also takes a discipline that is unique.

Principle #5 Compassion

Compassion is extremely important in becoming a leader and in developing new leaders for the next generation. Of all the soft skills I have written about, this is the most extreme soft skill, but a leader struggles without it because the essence of leadership is being able to develop more leaders. Without the leadership principle of compassion, a leader will struggle to develop others.

Compassion is a hard trait to exhibit in one's own culture and even more so in multiple cultures. How a global leader communicates with and treats the next generation of leaders is as important as the process. Inappropriate words or cultural insensitivities can cause a leader to be labeled as weak or hegemonistic. Both are damaging to relationships and decrease the effectiveness of leadership.

The final part of the book addresses the issues surrounding the development of global leaders. Development of cognitive complexity in leaders is wide ranging in research, but if global leadership is more complex than domestic leadership, how do organizations develop effective global leaders? By ensuring global leaders and followers understand the complexities and paradoxes of the context in which global work is done to improve practices and therefore leadership effectiveness.

I write about these important leadership principals as I have learned them from Arabs, Americans, Cambodians, Chinese, Europeans, Indians, and others to give current and future global leaders the ability to lead effectively and impact lives for the good of society. The leaders who use these principles when taking on challenges and objectives to move people forward will change generations for the better and help create a better place to live and work.

2

GLOBAL LEADERSHIP
AND COGNITIVE COMPLEXITY

My heart started racing when I realized the offensive mistake. The Palestinian refugees taking my English language class were whistling and shaking their heads no. I instantly knew what I had done wrong, and as I turned to look at the whiteboard, the cultural faux pas glared back at me. I had innocently highlighted a few vocabulary words listed on the board by placing a star next to them. I drew the stars like we did in my class back in America … with six points, just like the Jewish Star of David.

Though my class was understanding, and we had respect for each other, I knew there were members of Hamas in the group. It was early 2000, and the second intifada had just started. It was not a good time for an American to make any references to Israel. Each time I came to teach the class, the students escorted me from the entrance of the camp to the classroom and then back again to the taxi just to make sure I was safe. The political environment called for caution, not carelessness like making this type of mistake. In the end, they knew my motives were pure based on my character and integrity.

Fourteen years later, I can write about this story with amusement, but it's one of many instances where I've learned from failures as well as successes. From my experiences and study of global leadership dynamics, I've concluded most people do not understand the complexities and paradoxes that lie ahead when moving from domestic to global leadership.

Along with the Beatles, many singers and songwriters correctly communicate that what the world needs is love. To fulfill this need at the heart of every culture and person, the world needs loving leadership through effective global leadership. Love is an idle word that quickly fades unless a person envisions and shows others active love. This envisioning and consequent responsible action is leadership. Love and leadership share attributes because they are bound in action, and the focus is on others, at least it should be. We live in a world of 7 billion people. The world is hurting and needs love. Through effective global leadership, the world will receive this love.

Global Leadership Research

In their book, *The Global Leadership Challenge,* Morrison and Black (2014) used research spanning hundreds of organizations and global leaders over the last 20 years. They concluded only 18 percent of global organizations had the full capacity of global leaders needed for success of the organization. This means 82 percent of organizations were short on needed global leaders, ranging from a small deficit to a huge lack in global leadership.

Morrison and Black (2014) explored the reason for a shortage of global leaders in organizations. In a targeted study of 40 global human resource (HR) executives, Morrison and Black made four main conclusions for the lack of global leaders: (1) a fast-growing demand for global leaders, (2) majority of global leaders are needed in developing markets (not the easiest places to be relocated), (3) failure of organizations to identify the need for global leaders, and (4) executives who do not fully appreciate the time, training, and deliberately designed experience needed to develop global leaders.

These reasons align with my experiences over the past fifteen-plus years. I enjoy the complexities of meeting a need in a fast-growing industry. My background is developing global leaders in developing markets where there is the greatest need. I advocate for consulting with organizational leaders on the need to identify effective global leaders, and I advise that global leadership development is a deliberate process. My job is not training a hard skill but instead developing a leader to have bifocals through which he or she sees locally and globally with the same lens. There is not a clear process in place to accomplish this task, but that again is a thrilling part of the industry. As globalization changes societies, we are able to create and innovate in order to serve organizations by developing effective global leaders.

Before I can adequately describe the five principles and how they help with the complexities of global leadership, we first have to frame the concept. This is not an easy task because many people have many ideas about how to define global leadership and how it is practiced in the global market. Here is my definition of a global leader: a global leader is a person who leads across cultures to perform complex leadership with systems, processes, and relationships.

Following is a review of scholars trying to define global leadership.

Global Leadership Conceptual Framework

Due to the emergence of international business as separate from domestic business, the study of global leadership continues to gain attention. Even with this growing attention, empirical research is still lacking. Global leadership empirical research gained steam in the 1990s. From 2012-2014, an explosion of research has occurred with many empirical studies and conceptual articles published on global leadership. Although there is an increase of empirical research in global leadership, it is still far behind empirical studies in domestic leadership. Many academics see global leadership as simply one of many types of leadership. But global leadership isn't just one of many leadership styles. It is separate from theories like transformational and servant leadership. I agree with prominent researchers in the field like Bird, Mendehall, and Osland, who say global leadership research is separate from domestic leadership studies.

Although domestic and global leadership are two different umbrellas, the conceptual framework of global leadership studies is built upon the same foundational research of leadership theory. From general leadership theory comes the ability to define global leadership according to necessary leadership competencies. Therefore, having a greater knowledge and understanding of the foundation of general leadership theory leads to a more comprehensive and valid understanding of global leadership in its similarities and differences.

The beginnings of leadership theory can be traced back to Greek philosophy. In most cases, the leader was male. The Greek philosopher Plato described a leader as a philosopher-king. During the Renaissance, Machiavelli wrote *The Prince* that provided direction to political leaders. In modern philosophy, Nietzsche, who was a recognized philosopher of power, described the leader as Zarathustra, the character in his book who was a superman type of leader. Not until the twentieth century did leadership theorists begin using empirical research.

The great man theory of leadership reigned for thousands of years before Stodgill's (1948) research shed light on the person and abilities of the leader and on the leader's situation. Stodgill's research opened a door for Katz's research on leadership skills. Katz's theory was based on the three skills approach. The three personal skills for an effective administrator were technical, human, and conceptual.

The focus on the leader-follower relationship began with Fielder's (1971) research in contingency theory and with House's research in path-goal theory. Many changes in American culture took place in the 1970s, and leadership theory was not exempt from them. Hersey and Blanchard introduced situational leadership. For the first time, a leadership theory explored the development of followers.

Leadership traits have been a topic of research since the early 1900s. Zaccaro (2007) connected leadership traits to personal characteristics that improve leadership effectiveness in diverse groups and organizational situations. Zaccaro defined traits with two elements. The first element is that leadership traits are effective in organizations. The second element is that leadership traits work across many organizational situations.

Greenleaf (2002) wrote *The Servant as Leader,* a seminal essay on servant leadership. He pointed out that changes in the American culture in the 1970s forced leaders to adapt their leadership styles to focus on service. The core concept of servant leadership focuses on the change of the American institution or organization. Greenleaf spent most of his career working for AT&T, which was then the largest organization in the United

States. He saw that leaders needed to focus on how to more effectively serve followers instead of just building their own skills and abilities.

Another prevalent leadership theory is transformational leadership. Bass and Avolio (1994) developed the 4 I's to demonstrate the difference between transformational and transactional leadership. The 4 I's include idealized influence, inspirational motivation, intellectual stimulation, and individual consideration. They then listed four characteristics of a transformational leader that grew out of the 4 I's. A transformational leader does the following: (1) stimulates interest among colleagues and followers to view their work from other perspectives, (2) generates awareness of the mission or vision of the team and organization, (3) develops colleagues and followers to a higher level of ability and potential, and (4) motivates colleagues and followers to look beyond their interests toward those that will benefit the group.

As leadership theory progressed into the 1980s, the foundation of the theories was based on American research. Hofstede (1980) wrote a seminal article that challenged the thought process of how American leadership theories apply internationally. Hofstede established a large research project incorporating 40 independent nations to demonstrate how cultures differ. He found four criteria: power distance, uncertainty avoidance, individualism-collectivism, and masculinity-femininity.

Hofstede's research showed that "leadership in any culture … is a complement to subordinateship." Because of the cultural conditioning of their subordinates, leaders cannot choose their styles of leadership at will. Instead, they have to understand the cultural context in which they are leading and how the subordinates will receive the leadership style. For this reason, Hofstede recommended Fiedler's contingency theory as an effective style of leadership across cultures.

Hofstede laid the foundation for the global leadership conceptual framework, but the complexities of global leadership increased from the time of Hofstede's (1980) research with the explosion of globalization in the early 1990s. Just as leadership theory has problems establishing a conceptual framework due to having over 200 definitions, global leadership theory has difficulties with a conceptual framework due to a plethora of definitions.

Defining Global Leadership

A lack of clarity and the degree of confusion in the global leadership construct is the biggest obstacle in global leadership research. One of the earliest construct definitions for global leadership started in the late 1990s with Spreitzer, McCall, and Mahoney (1997) and continued with Gregersen, Morrison, and Black (1998) and Petrick, Scherer, Brodzinski, Quinn, and Ainina (1999).

Spreitzer, et al. (1997) researched the traditional approach to the identification process for international executives. The research drew from literature and produced a reliable measurement tool to rate potential global leaders. Spreitzer, et al. (1997) defined the international executive as a person who has a role with international responsibilities.

Gregersen, et al. (1998) focused their construct on the development of global leaders. In the research, 136 executives in 50 global organizations completed interviews. The second aspect of the research was surveying 108 Fortune 500 companies in the United States. The definition of global leader used in the interview was a leader who can guide an organization that spans across countries, cultures, and customers.

Petrick, et al. (1999) proposed that global leadership skills assisted organizations in sustaining a competitive advantage. Petrick defined the practice of global leadership as the enhancement of the organization through strategic thinking in order to increase the competiveness of the organization. The research identified four areas where a global leader increases the competitive advantage of an organization. They are profitability and productivity, continuity and efficiency, commitment and morale, and adaptability and innovation.

As the 21st century began, researchers more vigorously pursued a construct definition of global leadership. In the 2000s, McCall and Hollenbeck (2002) argued for complexity in the construct of global leadership. McCall and Hollenbeck claimed the definition of global leader is more than just a leader who crosses cultural boundaries. There has to be a layer of complexity added to the act of leading across cultures and borders.

Suutari (2002) focused the research on global leader development. From a review of literature, Suutari identified that there was still not a clear definition of global leader. Without a clear definition of global leadership, organizations are hindered in the development of global leaders. Suutari chose to define global leaders as those having a global integration of responsibilities in global organizations.

As the global economy continued to grow, organizations became more aware of the need to develop global leaders. To define global leaders, Caligiuri (2006) explained that global leaders are leaders in international jobs that manage in a complex, changing, and often ambiguous global environment. The research identified ten tasks that separate a global leader from a domestic leader. The tasks are to work with teams across cultures, interact with external and internal clients from diverse countries, speak a second language, supervise employees from different cultures, develop a global strategic plan, manage a worldwide budget, negotiate with people in other countries, manage foreign vendors, and manage worldwide risks.

A move to predicting global leader effectiveness came about at the end of the first decade of the 21st Century. To predict effectiveness, there has to be a construct of the definition of a global leader. Caligiuri and Tarique (2009) defined global leaders as top-level professionals who play an important role in creating and sustaining a competitive advantage. The study of over 200 global leaders found that high-contact, cross-cultural leadership development experiences and leaders' personalities were ways to predict global leader effectiveness. Caligiuri and Tarique concluded that a highly extroverted leader with greater high-contact, cross-cultural leadership development experience is the most effective in global leadership practices.

Patterson, Dannhauser, and Stone (2007) viewed global leadership uniquely. Global is a singular term that includes the world. Patterson concluded that "global leaders are challenged to create new models of management systems, not just by being innovative and recognizing individual contributions, but also by taking into account the cross-cultural aspects of different societies" (Patterson et al., 2007, p.8).

In an attempt to construct a definition of global leadership that is the most comprehensive, Mendenhall et al. (2012) reviewed and critiqued existing definitions. Using the previous 20 global leader constructs, Mendenhall separated the definitions into the categories of a state, a process, or both. The state of global leadership is grouped by specific tasks, activities, and job responsibilities. The process of global leadership is how leaders engage and fulfill their roles. The engagement includes sense-making, quality of relationships, and the tools used to influence followers.

After reviewing and categorizing definitions, the second step of the research clarified the global construct. Mendenhall (2012) constructed three dimensions of global leadership. They are complexity, flow, and presence. Because of the desire to separate from past definitions that offered circular arguments, Mendenhall constructed two definitions, one definition for global leadership and another definition for global leader.

Holt and Seki (2012) offer a differing view on the process of global leadership. The major difference in their construct is that global leaders need to add more than just competencies. In order to be effective as a global leader, the future global leader has to make major developmental shifts. The developmental shifts are in multicultural effectiveness, adeptness at managing paradoxes, cultivation of the "being" dimension of human experience, and appreciation of individual uniqueness in the context of cultural differences.

Holt and Seki's (2012) study of global leaders spanned over 250 individuals who were either interviewed or surveyed to demonstrate the developmental shift in global leadership. From their research conclusions, Holt and Seki made two statements that separated their research from others in global leadership. The first statement is that globalization goes back thousands of years, and the basic concepts or principles of leadership are universal and timeless. The second statement proposed that a huge shift in leadership research is underway that will define all leaders as global. Holt and Seki defined global leadership as "anyone who operates in a context of multicultural, paradoxical complexity to achieve results in our world."

The various definitions of global leadership range from describing it as a state, a process, or both. Some authors such as Caligiuri and Osland present multiple articles to define global leadership. The multiple definitions for global leadership prove the lack of clarity in global leadership research. To help clarify the actions of a global leader, I will review literature on global leadership competencies.

Global Leadership Competencies

Developing a list of global leadership competencies is similar to constructing a definition of global leadership. Bird (2013) listed 160 separate global leadership competencies referred to in journal articles from 1993-2012. Adler and Bartholomew (1992), Wills and Barham (1992), Jokinen (2005), Tubbs and Shulz (2006), Gitsham (2008), and Bird (2013) are some of the foundational researchers on global leadership competencies referred to in these articles.

Adler and Bartholomew (1992) surveyed 50 major North American firms in the early 1990s. The findings were focused on the fact that not all companies are the same globally; meaning, the environment, location, and type of service are different. At that time because many companies were moving into trans-national business, their human resource strategy was lagging behind their global business strategy. Adler and Bartholomew (1992) identified the following trans-national skills: global perspective, synergistic learning, transition and adaption, cross-cultural interaction, collaboration, and foreign experience.

Will and Barham (1992) also attempted to describe global leadership competencies. They studied sixty international managers in different countries and industries. From surveying leadership competency and skills, three major interlinking parts were found. The parts were cognitive complexity, emotional energy, and psychological maturity. An international manager showed effectiveness when he had high competencies in these three areas.

By 2005, research on global leadership competencies finally had enough empirical research to review and compile a more integrated framework (Jokinen, 2005). The new framework by Jokinen (2005) consisted of three dimensions. The first dimension was entitled core of global leadership competencies, and it included self-awareness, engagement in personal transformation, and inquisitiveness. The second dimension referred to the desired mental characteristics of global leaders, which included optimism, self-regulation, social judgment skills, and tangible knowledge. The third dimension was the desired behavioral competencies of global leaders, which included social skills, networking skills, and knowledge.

Tubbs and Schulz (2006) explored the taxonomy of global leadership competencies and meta-competencies. Tubbs and Schulz identified 50 global leadership competencies from the taxonomy. Tubbs also utilized his 35 years of research of over 50,000 global leaders from various continents and industries. From this research, they narrowed the competencies to seven behaviors of an effective global leader: 1) understanding the big picture, 2) attitudes are everything 3) leadership, the driving force, 4) communication, the leader's voice, 5) innovation and creativity, 6) leading change, and 7) teamwork and followership.

Bird (2013) mapped out the domain of global leadership competencies. He pointed out that global competencies do not look different from other lists of leadership competencies, but it is the multiplicity, notion of interdependence, and ambiguity of these competencies that separate the global leader from the domestic leader.

Bird (2013) explained that research on global leadership is not for the purpose of creating new leadership competencies for global leaders but for pointing out that although competencies are the same as for a domestic leader, the complexities of leadership increase for global leaders. With added complexity comes the need for specific knowledge and different skills to successfully navigate and lead in global organizations.

What are the complexities in global leadership?

Now that the definition and competencies of global leadership are established, it is important to report research on complexity and global leadership. Gitsham (2008) conducted research of 33 CEOs and HR specialists during a United Nations Global Compact Conference. The research listed three basic skill sets needed for a global leader. The skill sets are context, complexity, and connectedness. Context is the ability of the global leader to understand and respond to changes in the external environment. Complexity is the ability to survive and thrive in situations of limited information. Connectedness is the ability of a global leader to build effective relationships with new partners.

Similar to Wills and Barham (1992), Dragoni and McAlpine (2012) believed cognitive complexity is a critical competency of a global leader.

Dragoni and McAlpine claimed that global leaders not only have to manage relationships with diverse cultures, but they also need to lead the business. Global leaders are required to have high cognitive complexity to "synthesize this disparate knowledge that can give rise to innovative ways to respond to local demands while leveraging global opportunities and resources."

Global leaders not only have to manage relationships with diverse cultures, but they also need to lead the business. Global leaders are required to have a high cognitive complexity to "synthesize this disparate knowledge that can give rise to innovative ways to respond to local demands while leveraging global opportunities and resources."

Cognitive complexity is more than just a theory. It also holds weight on the practical aspect of leadership. Below are the five principles along with a brief summary of how they are part of the complexities in global leadership.

How do the five principles connect to cognitive complexity?

Instead of trying to explain 160 global leadership competencies, I am reducing the framework to the five principles. A number of competencies are birthed within these principles, but these five foundational principles are most important for a global leader to exhibit.

1. Integrity

Moore and Tenbrunsel (2014) researched the impact of moral reasoning on cognitively complex situations. Overall, the research showed that more reasoning provided sub-optimal outcomes for cognitive complex situations. A leader has to find moderate reasoning to be effective in complex situations. If the leader reasons too much or thinks too little, it is detrimental. The goal is for the leader to find motivation to make a rational decision based on the complexity in order to move past self-interested choices.

Global leadership is complex, and cognitive complexity is a daily issue when dealing with moral choices such as hiring/firing, partnerships, choosing vendors, and marketing to donors. All of these situations are complex and require moral choices. The challenge for you as a leader is to make sure you spend enough time understanding the consequences of your moral choice and yet not allow yourself to spend too much time reasoning on the moral choice that it keeps you from making a clear and concise decision.

2. Passion

Cognitive complexity in global leadership does not just mean everything is more complicated. Cognitive complexity is when solutions are needed in an environment of uncertainty with a lack of problem-solving processes. It is in the complexity that the vision and passion of the global leader is tested in the crucible of uncertainties.

Vision casting for a global leader is outside the current frame of reference. No benchmark or template is established for how the process has been done in the past. The global leader's passion builds endurance to solve complex problems for the organization. The solutions will come from an openness to experience success and failure.

3. Sacrifice

If a person reads through biographies of global leaders, it is easy to see sacrifice. Smith and Lewis (2011) explain that "cognitive complexity allows leaders to explore contradictions in hopes of identifying new possibilities and reframing existing mindsets" (p.229). The ability to identify new possibilities and reframe existing mindsets comes about in tension or conflict. A global leader does not build a barrier around his or her ideas but instead sees tension as the ability to build something new.

When discussing sacrifice and global leadership, the first place to start is with leading self. To manage the complexities of global leadership, the leader is challenged in self-motivation to adapt in a life of ambiguous circumstances. Self-leadership also incorporates the sacrifice of the family as they are moved around the world to fulfill the vision. After self-leadership, humility of the global leader is the last part of sacrifice that manages complexity in global leadership. This is not just personal humility but also organizational humility.

4. Discipline

In today's global economy, change occurs at a frightening pace. A global leader has to be disciplined to manage the speed of change. Leadership is understanding oneself and also assessing follower performance. One of the key areas requiring high performance in today's organizations is change. For this reason, the ability to create and lead successful change projects is critical for a leader.

5. Compassion

Compassion is not a word often used to describe effective leadership, but looking deeper into explanations of complexity shows that exhibiting compassion is critical for a global leader. The Complex Leadership Theory identified not only systems as complex but also relationships as a complexity.

The complexity in global leadership is nonlinear and unpredictable. A global leader has to show compassion in developing complex relationship among diverse people. If the leader is rigid and completely linear in relationships, people will be hesitant to follow. To help a global leader manage this complexity, he or she has to develop compassion through sensemaking. Leaders use sensemaking when a current situation is different from an expected situation. Sensemaking is implemented by noticing and bracketing, labeling, and organizing through communication using retrospection, presumption, social and systematic teamwork, and action.

Going Forward

We have identified that cognitive complexity is a critical competency for global leaders. Now what? Unfortunately, there is still much debate on if a person can develop cognitive complexity. Therefore, the remainder of the book illustrates the importance of the five principles of effective global leadership and suggests ways to develop these principles to manage the complexities in the global workplace.

The essence of global leadership is its complexities, and the personal stories at the beginning of each chapter illustrate this fact. By developing the five principles of effective global leadership, a global leader will manage the complexities more effectively, grow into a more responsible leader, and help give the world its essential need: love.

Part 2

The Five Principles Of Global Leadership

3

INTEGRITY

I was a defeated man. For seven years I had worked hard and sacrificed much to start and grow a consulting company. Many doubted our expansion into China because small consulting firms do not fit into China's business model. We focused for three years on China and had acquired clients from medium-sized manufactures to large state-owned organizations. Life was good. I was being driven around China in black Audis and staying in five-star hotels.

Suddenly, our success came to a screeching halt. We were in the process of finalizing a long-term leadership development project to train 500 middle-level managers over the next five years. This was the big break we were waiting for, but the devastating Sichuan earthquake in 2008 caused many of our clients to place development projects on hold. Large corporations often experience delays, but for small organizations delays are a threat to the organization's existence. I exhausted every possibility and even leveraged my personal credit to keep cash flow available and wait out the delays.

In the midst of these events, my health became an added struggle. I had two lithotripsy procedures in Hong Kong for large kidney stones due to working, traveling, and dehydrating. I was in physical pain and mental anguish. We returned to the U.S. to make sure my procedures were successful and learned I needed a third procedure to remove a stone that was still lodged. This procedure was the most painful of them all.

My credit line was dwindling, a global crisis was brewing, and my health was failing. As I sat on the floor of my in-law's house, I received a call on Skype from China. It was one of my largest client's former employees. He offered me a deal. Although it was in the grey area (not technically illegal in China but definitely immoral), I knew it was not a deal that fit into my ethical code of conduct. Even though I desperately needed the cash - and it was going to bring in a very large sum, I knew it was not the right thing to do.

I am not alone in this dilemma. Many, if not most, global leaders are faced with similar situations on a regular basis. When leading organizations around the world, a time will come when cultures collide, and a question of integrity is asked. At this point a global leader must understand the responsibility to the greater good of the community and the world. The decisions leaders make have a ripple effect in their own lives and in those of their families, businesses, and communities.

The core value of leadership, or for anything in life, is integrity. This is why integrity is the first principle in the foundation of managing the complexities of global leadership. Morrison and Black (2014) used the word *character* as an essential element of global leadership, but there needs to be a stronger word, one that has a universal standard. Looking deeper for a universal higher moral standard, you find integrity.

Leaders are the most successful when they are walking the path of integrity, and they will see their demise when they select the path of crookedness. This scenario has been played and replayed in the American corporate world. We ask the question: How do we form a business model that can help restore trust in corporate America? The answer to this question is very simple. Executives must make decisions with integrity and build a true image based on a foundation of company beliefs and values. It is not enough to bring in an auditing team or a group of attorneys to make sure you technically did not break the law. In business schools there is always a debate on ethical and legal decisions. Business decisions are not always black and white so we must draw the line. When making crucial decisions regarding ethical and legal issues, leaders need strong personal values to guide them.

First, a leader must form definitions and applications for the word *integrity*. In order for a leader to have followers, a leader must establish some standard of truth. There has to be a basis on which a leader makes decisions. Integrity by definition is "steadfast adherence to a strict ethical code." (The American Heritage College Dictionary, Third Edition, 1993)

> A man might himself know too little, perform poorly, lack judgment and ability, and yet not do damage as a manager. But if he has a lack in character and integrity—no matter how knowledgeable, how brilliant, how successful – destroys. He destroys people, the most valuable resource of the enterprise. He destroys spirit. And he destroys performance (Drucker, 1986).

Principle #1 Integrity

Adheres to, and acts in alignment with, a set of core values and beliefs; keeps his/her word and commitments; establishes credibility with others by 'walking the talk'; provides honest feedback in an appropriate and helpful manner; admits mistakes; doesn't misrepresent self for personal gain; maintains confidentiality; is seen as a truthful and trustworthy leader.

In global leadership, your character is tested on a regular basis. Each crisis of leadership will require a global leader to decipher core values from cultural values. Before you can decipher these differences, you must have a clear understanding of your own core values.

Complexities in Moral Choice

Global leaders are faced on a daily basis with moral choices. Most are more subtle than the obvious bribery and thievery. The grey areas include which supplier to choose (low cost or environmentally friendly), what partnership to develop (more revenue or better reputation), and who to hire and fire (give a woman a three-month maternity leave or fire her when she becomes pregnant). These choices seem easy on the surface, but for many global leaders, cultural differences in how they view each situation give them added complexity.

Moore and Tenbrunsel (2014) described this cognitive complexity and moral choice in their research on moral development theory. They researched the moral choice for decision makers and how much time decision makers reasoned about the problem. The research concluded that there was a "just enough" amount of time for reasoning, and decision makers who thought too little or too much made poorer moral choices.

The research by Moore and Tenbrunsel (2014) sheds light on one of many complexities faced by global leaders when dealing with integrity. Along with how much time to reason on moral choices, global leaders have to determine how to use and disperse power and knowledge, how to disseminate information, and to whom and when to communicate critical knowledge.

How to manage complexities through integrity?

As leadership research continues to move from an individual process to a collaborative process, the transformation places a larger emphasis on the values of the leader. If leaders desire to leave a legacy, there is a right and wrong way to leave your mark. The legacy depends not on your bank account when you die but the process in which you made decisions as a leader. "Leaders are people who have an unusual degree of power to create the conditions under which other people must live and move and have their being, conditions that can either be as illuminating as heaven or as shadowy as hell"(Johnson, 2009, p. 233). A more theoretical term used to describe the decisions, actions, and conditions is *ethics*. To understand the depth of the word *integrity*, we have to examine ethics in leadership, specifically, how context and culture impact ethics for a global leader.

Many theorists believe ethics is the heart of leadership, but when people hear the word *ethics,* they only think about the utilization of money. In actuality your ethics guide you in situations such as communication to employees, work ethic, and character in the field. To understand how integrity manages complexity of a global leader, it is important to look at why leaders choose not to demonstrate integrity, situational ethics, and context and culture impacting ethics.

Why do leaders choose not to demonstrate integrity?

To manage the complexities of global leadership, the ability to lead with integrity is critical. Most leaders would agree with this, so we need to understand why leaders choose not to live with integrity. Moral leadership research shows that most people have universal moral principles in their ethical belief systems, but when placed in certain situations, leaders can lose sight of these moral principles. Highly stressful situations, such as time pressure, keeping one's job, and stakeholder demands, create an uncertainty that can change the ethical judgment of global leaders.

In Luban's (2006) research on moral judgment, he gives four primary situations that could cause a leader to change their ethical practices.

1. Executive Position: This territory is what Luban (2006) calls "highly adversarial settings" (p.59). He contends that cultures like American society do not have clear ethical standards for behavior in highly competitive settings. "That implies a lot of moral uncertainty and ambiguity in a culture as addicted to competition as ours is" (p.61).
2. Competitive Environment: Another challenge to an ethical code is most cultures love winners and hate losers. Luban (2006) states that "given the choice between breaking the rules and winning or being a law-abiding loser (p.63)" many in a competitive culture choose to win at all costs. Many people view this as necessary carnage in the competitive marketplace but do not feel the same when the carnage is relationships, people's livelihood, and safety.
3. Achieving Financial Goals: Economics is the next dimension that challenges the global leader's integrity in decision making. Being successful in the system of large corporations that requires predictions with huge chunks of information is extremely difficult. "It does not matter how smart executives are or how fast on their feet. The world around them is faster" (Rhode, 2006, p.64). Because executives cannot predict success in our fast-paced world, they tend to cover up, lie, or shift blame for their mistakes.
4. Decisions for the Collective: The final dimension is a leader's cognitive dissonance and moral compass. Luban (2006) describes

cognitive dissonance as a process when our beliefs change with our conduct. Along with this description, he provides an illustration of a compass. Our morality is stronger when faced with individual decisions, but when placed in a group, research shows morality differs based on pressures from the group. For this reason, leaders can influence followers in corporations to lie, mismanage, and cover up unethical actions.

Most global leaders do not start out thinking they will make unethical decisions, but the complexity of their role brings it about. These four dimensions describe critical areas where leaders choose to lose their integrity. This is a good beginning, but a deeper understanding of situational ethics will help to successfully manage the complexities of leading with integrity.

Situational Ethics: Communication

An essential part of being a leader with character integration is telling the truth. Cloud (2006) calls this the Truth 101. When we are deceptive, it "usually makes us incur more negative consequences than if we had told the truth" (p.103). In any situation, the probability of success is better when you tell the truth. The truism seems simple, but the practicality is complex in leadership.

When motivation turns into manipulation, deceit is usually in the mix. Although a leader starts with telling the truth, being in touch with reality takes more than just telling the truth. A leader has to go deeper and identify the traits of a truthful character.

Leaders wish decisions were based on the simple black and white truth, but most of the time, the truth is not simple. Leaders can fall under their own trances and unintentionally deceive followers. In Dr. Henry Cloud's (2006) book *Integrity*, he said, "The reason is not that they are lying, but that they miss parts of reality that are important to making things work. In the kind of successful character that we are talking about here, the integrated or 'whole' character, a grasp of truth is always present and increasing, which requires some specific traits" (p.105). The core trait is reality. A leader has to understand that reality is always your friend.

In the plethora of meetings on vision, mission, and purpose, leaders spend so much time thinking five years down the road that they lose sight of reality. Their minds are in another location focused on the future, and they forget about the day-to-day problems. So leaders have to find ways to develop character integration that allow them to keep in touch with reality, starting with the situation the organization is in presently. This type of situational ethics is critical for the success of an organizational leader.

A leader with character integration is one who seeks reality. The ability to seek reality has a foundation in humility. Cloud explains most leaders don't seek reality with humility; "many people, because of pride or narcissism, or just bullheadedness, approach a task like that and basically say, 'Get out of my way. I know what I am doing'" (p.112).

By being delusional and afraid of reality and truth, a leader's character suffers. Cloud describes four primary character issues that become barriers to character integration:

1. Fear of being wrong.
2. A false fixed view of self from the past. This could be negative or positive.
3. Limited skills and resources to meet the challenges of the organization.
4. Finding out a person has to redo a life plan or script because he or she was misled.

In contrast, a leader with integrity is a person who seeks out reality about the current situation and has the strength and courage to assess whatever real information he finds. This type of character demonstrates the courage to meet reality. Two ways a leader demonstrates character integration through being in touch with reality and people are balancing emotion and judgment and the ability to assimilate and accommodate.

Cloud (2006) claims that the human body has two minds. One is emotional feeling and the other is rational thought. The temptation for leaders is to fall on one side, but a leader with character integration understands how to balance both sides. The drive for character development comes from a passion or emotion that has to be balanced with clear judgment of reality for whole character integration.

The second demonstration of character integration is the ability to assimilate and accommodate. This is opposite of saying a leader is always right and anything outside of his or her world of thinking is wrong or untrue. The process of making external reality an internal reality is called assimilation and accommodation. By growing in this character trait, leaders are able to assimilate information.

After the leader takes in the new information or true reality, he accommodates this new view into his own thinking. Many skills are needed to assimilate and accommodate, but "cognitive and emotional flexibility is key for fluid performance and negotiating reality" (Cloud, 2006, p. 138). With huge amounts of data in today's world, global leaders have to develop the ability to see new realities and grow in character integration. Through this growth they can meet the personal challenges of the 21st century. A global leader grows in character integration by understanding context and culture.

Context and Challenges to Moral Leadership

Much of a leader's success is contributed to understanding the context in which the process of leadership is undertaken. For global leaders, the complexity is that context can change between two conversations because of diversity, ambiguity and location of the leadership process. For this reason, a global leader has to understand the challenges of the context in moral leadership. There are three primary ways to categorize the context: time, ambivalence, and sense of self.

1. Time: According to Margolis and Molinsky (2006), time management can impact morals on either side of the spectrum. Too little time or too much time opens up opportunities for unethical practices, but for executives and professionals in organizations, it is the time squeeze that causes the most problems. To offset the temptation for unethical behavior due to limited time, a moral leader has to "be cognizant of time and manage it actively rather than just lament its swift passage" (Rhode, 2006, p.82).

2. Ambivalence: "Moral leadership often requires people to act in a manner they sense is right even as it unleashes uneasiness and

misgiving" (Rhode, 2006, p.84). Margolis and Molinsky (2006) pointed out that moral leaders act responsibly and for the greater good of their followers during this challenge. They detail two ways ambivalence encourages moral leadership: 1)moral leaders keep track of "residue" from their decisions and know what will happen to others because of their decisions, 2)"ambivalence sustains moral sensibility and guards against callousness" (p.88).

3. Sense of Self: Moral leaders have a sense of how their actions impact others. The description is similar to self-awareness in emotional intelligence. Leaders have a sense of fairness and equality that allows them to measure the effect of decisions to various degrees. "A sense of self that tells us we are responsible... may be crucial for those moments when moral leadership is most needed" (Rhode, 2006, p.93).

The context of time and ambivalence is played out in the use and disbursement of power. How a global leader chooses to demonstrate integrity through moral challenges is centered on the ability to manage power in order to show trust and humility. Within the context of power is the complexity for global leaders to also understand culture. When global leaders have to mix context and culture with power, sense of self is critical for the global leader to reduce this highly complex situation.

Context: Power and Leadership

Why is ethical leadership and integrity complex in global leadership? The complexity lies with how the global leader distributes, uses, and demonstrates power during crisis and conflict. Don't assume only destructive consequences in crisis and conflict. We will also explore constructive consequences of both while we build a foundational knowledge of power and leadership.

One of the primary reasons global leaders are measured by their integrity is because they possess a large amount of power across cultures and countries. Even a small organization in the U.S. that is purchasing and selling its products overseas can influence the community with which they are operating. A small business owner in the U.S. can become enamored with power when traveling to a community that treats him like royalty in order to keep his business. Many theorists believe leadership and power are intertwined and cannot be separated. For this reason it is important to understand the good and the bad of power in leadership.

Leadership and power are directly related. Companies face challenges developing leaders with integrity because authority systems change quickly, and the global economy is moving from a triangle hierarchy to a flat organizational structure. With the increased information provided by technology, having power through the control of knowledge is getting increasingly harder.

In the modern organizations of the Industrial Age, power was controlled by limiting knowledge and information to a privileged few. Morgan (2006) stated that "by controlling these key resources a person can systematically influence the definition of the organizational situations and can create patterns of dependency." Whether the term "gatekeeper" or "power broker" is used, the same result happens. By blocking knowledge a person can become an "expert" and make followers dependent.

> Team-based organization typically increases the adaptability of organizations in dealing with their environments, improves coordination between functional specialisms, and makes good use of human resources. The approach also diffuses influence and control, allowing people at the middle and lower levels of an organization to make contributions that might otherwise be denied. (Morgan, 2006, p.53)

In today's knowledge organizations, global leaders struggle to correctly manage power with followers. A complexity for global leaders is the aspect of integrity and power. The question is how does the global leader manage the power distance with followers?

Power Distance

When discussing power in organizations, one of the first researchers of global management, Dr. Hofstede, segmented four dimensions of national culture:

1. Power Distance
2. Uncertainty Avoidance
3. Individualism-Collectivism
4. Masculinity-Femininity.

The dimension labeled power distance is the extent to which a society accepts that power in institutions and organizations is distributed unequally. More recent research found that followers give over power to the leaders for decisions to be made. Organizations with higher amounts of power distance develop obedient employees who do not openly challenge the decisions of the upper management. Organizations with a lower score of power distance have more autonomous decision making with followers freely communicating opinions to upper management.

If you are leading a team of people from both China and the U.S., that team has the complexity of power distance. The Chinese are accustomed to being obedient followers and easily give power over to leaders. An American is taught independence from an early age and feels he or she can give feedback to decisions and should operate with limited power distance. When people from these two cultures are co-workers, how do you lead this team?

Organizational Power and Performance

Yukl (2010) uses the term *influence* to explain power of leaders in organizations. He researches how top executives "influence the financial performance and survival of an organization" (p.708). Servant leadership theory accounts for the leader sharing power and interacting to influence performance. Some propositions by Yukl synthesize with servant leadership, such as organizational performance determinants. Leaders can influence the performance of organizations by relevant behaviors, such as task-oriented, relations-oriented, and change-oriented behaviors.

Leaders use their power to influence performance and also to influence structural forms. There are many forms of structure, but an effective one for leadership is how power and information is distributed in the organization. Many look to the heroic leader to make all decisions, which harms the organization. Distributing the decision-making, power, and relationships in the organization gives the leader greater ability to increase the performance of the organization.

Culture: Power and Relationships

The culture in which a global leader distributes power is a vital piece of information. In essence, power is the relationship among persons. "To define power not as a property or entity or possession but as a *relationship* in which two or more persons tap motivational bases in one another and bring varying resources to bear in the process is to perceive power as drawing a vast range of human behavior into its orbit" (Burns, 1979, p.15). Power and relationships are extremely important for global leaders because trust is usually built virtually and not in many face-to-face meetings. The important part of power and relationships is seeing the role of the leader as power wielder in the culture.

"Power wielders draw from their power bases resources relevant to their own motives and resources of others upon whom they exercise power" (Burns, 1979, p.17) Leaders who exercise power through their authority in today's organizations see a different follower than those in the past of the modern world. Today, organizations also face a power struggle with leaders with authority as "power left unchecked drives leaders to divest scarce organizational resources away from collective purposes and toward endeavors that benefit themselves" (Rus, Van Knippenberg, & Wisse, 2012, p. 17).

The actions of leaders in organizations that abuse power create destructive patterns. The destruction can not only effect motivation of employees but lead to much larger issues such as ethical and moral failures. One of the areas where global leaders can potentially abuse power is in a crisis. During a crisis period, organizations look to the leader for solutions, and communication moves to a more centralized authoritative structure. As more power and responsibility move up to the leader, the more integrity the leader needs to make the right decisions.

One of the most prevalent displays of power in organizations is when they are facing crisis events. The added difficulty and lack of knowledge communicated during crisis management force leaders to make decisions without adequate information. Leaders are often forced to make critical decisions on limited information with many pressures from time and followers.

During a crisis event, organizations develop characteristics that define their actions. The first characteristic is probability. What is the probability an organization will undergo a certain crisis event? The second characteristic is impact. If a certain crisis event happens to an organization, what type of damage happens to the organization's goals and vision? The third characteristic is predictability. An organization tries to predict the crisis event by preparing for different scenarios. With the complexities of global leadership, a leader with integrity will understand the three characteristics and how to lead through the crisis. In the end when the crisis is finished, will the leaders return power distance to the previous levels? The following case study focuses on an organization's ability to develop global leaders with integrity and to manage power effectively during crisis and conflict.

LESSONS FROM A GLOBAL LEADER

The core lesson in Leadership 101 is there will be crisis. Synonymous with crisis is conflict. Global leaders will face conflict, and their integrity is tested by how they manage the conflict through sharing power, knowledge, and influence while still respecting other cultures and overcoming the complexities in the crisis.

A global leader with integrity embraces conflict and sees the situation as an opportunity for growth, both personally and organizationally. *Conflict is when people have differences in opinion, processes, beliefs, and allegiances and act on those differences with arguments and avoidance, which causes a disturbance in the processes in the system.*

The complexity for a global leader is when a conflict is between cultures, countries, and beliefs. The global leader must understand the conflict and know what is driving the conflict depending on cultural and philosophical differences. The first step is to decipher what is a good and bad conflict. Destructive conflict is one that destroys peace in the team and organization. The destructive conflict brings disunity along with hurt, shame, and anger.

In contrast, constructive conflict is essential to the growth of a global leader. During constructive conflict the leader learns to empower others to create ideas in a safe environment. The safe environment is built on trust. Trust is built on integrity and acting within ethical boundaries during conflict. To demonstrate the process, the case study below details the complexities for global leaders to lead with integrity. The challenge is balancing power distance while communicating during the conflict.

Background

Compassion Care Mission (CCM) is located in India. Their primary focus is on serving children by improving their health and education. With their expansion over the last 20 years, CCM has seen multiple executive directors fail. Much of the failure is centered on the lack of strategic leadership to lead a larger organization. For this reason, the following case study details a leadership development process to improve strategic leadership by developing conflict competent leaders who learn the skill of constructive behaviors.

In the progression of developing conflict competent leaders, the first task is to learn more about CCM. Currently CCM serves around 5,000 poor and needy children on a daily basis. They are a primary partner to a large multinational relief organization, so if a person adopts a child in India through this organization then there is a good chance that CCM is the one taking care of the child. Even with this success, CCM is still searching for a clear vision in going forward. One of the most challenging issues is their neglect to utilize conflict as a positive force to drive new innovation and services for children.

Because of the cultural differences within the organization, CCM needs to develop conflict competent leaders throughout the organization. To accomplish this they will need to train individuals and teams and create an integrated conflict management system for the entire organization. One of the primary goals of the developmental process is to introduce CCM to the need for constructive controversy through active and passive constructive behavior when dealing with conflict. From their development in these areas, CCM will create new programs and projects to expand their services to the poor and uneducated children in India.

Developing an Individual Conflict Competent Leader

"Leaders are expected to spot opportunities and problems quickly, act on them in the moment, and show results instantly. But when those opportunities and problems are conflict related, speed and immediacy are not necessary virtues" (Runde & Flanagan, 2013, p.97).

Leaders must understand that an estimated 20-40 percent of their time is spent dealing with conflict (Runde & Flanagan, 2013). Leaders with conflict competence have skills "to improve their personal ability to manage conflict" (Runde & Flanagan, 2013, p. 23). A leader has to develop certain skills, such as active listening, obtaining feedback, and critical thinking, to grow as a conflict competent leader.

"Constructive controversy occurs when even though a person's ideas or opinions are incompatible with another's, the two seek to reach an agreement or resolution" (p.172). The leader does not try to stop conflict but instead learns to manage conflict. A conflict competent leader manages conflict constructively in the following five ways:

1. The ability to be critical of ideas, not people.
2. The ability to separate issues of personal worth from criticism of one's ideas.
3. An uncompromising focus on best outcomes, not winning.

4. Listening to others' ideas
5. Efforts to understand all sides of issues (p.173).

Team Unity through Conflict

Runde and Flanagan (2013) discuss the idea of teams establishing an agreement. The agreement is to establish norms for addressing and managing conflict. "Conflict competent leaders take extra steps to help their teams take advantage of conflicting thoughts, feelings, ideas and perspectives" (p.223).

One challenge in CCM is their lack of creativity. Much of the problem stems from not setting the right climate in the team to use conflict as an opportunity for growth. "Creating the right climate means establishing a team environment that's conducive to honest discussions and colorful debates while preserving safety for all members" (p.224). The following are steps to help CCM start developing a team environment that is creative through conflict. These steps provided by Runde and Flanagan (2013) are very helpful in developing a conflict competent leader.

Step 1: The team needs to review the short-term mission and goals.
Step 2: Discuss the desired climate. How will the team work the most effectively?
Step 3: Brainstorm suggestions and ideas for creating the desired climate.
Step 4: List the "rules of conflict" for the team to review.
Step 5: Record and distribute the resulting list for review, or post on the conference room wall.

Development by training about power

Once leaders assess their individual hot button topics, build a conflict team agreement. The final step is to establish an organizational system to develop conflict competent leaders. "Conflict competent leadership requires championing a company-wide policy on conflict management" (p.257).

For CCM, having a developed conflict competent leader is critical as they prepare to change their top management team. Because of the executive director's retirement and the need to develop future leaders, CCM is creating an executive team. For the development of conflict competent leaders, this team needs to model effective disbursement of power during conflict for the rest of the organization. "In order to enjoy the full benefits that come from handling conflict effectively, leaders also champion the development of conflict competence throughout the organization" (p.251).

Since "structural and cultural aspects of organizations can influence how conflicts arise and unfold" (p.91), CCM needs to take the opportunity to build more constructive conflict in the organization. The challenges for growth are forcing CCM to become more creative with their programs, processes, and operations. For an organization like CCM, the desire to build conflict competent leaders is present, but the awareness of how to develop these leaders is not prevalent.

Situational Analysis

The suggestion for CCM is to use their senior leadership team as the task force. The reason is the leaders in this team must first learn to develop their conflict competence, and then they can assist in developing the leaders to manage conflict with staff, communities, and international partnerships. Since all organizations have their own DNA, there is not an off-the-shelf solution in creating an effective conflict competent leader. The following are the most pressing challenges for the leaders in handling of power.

Relationship with Board

To this point, CCM has been run by a powerful board that has demanded full compliance throughout the organization. Because of this demand, CCM leaders have not been inspired to prevent, identify, and resolve problems during conflict. The newly appointed senior leadership team will need to learn to navigate the relationship with the board in order to lead with integrity. Running from conflict and problems is an abuse of power just like being over controlling. How can the senior leaders learn to manage the conflict in order to grow the organization?

The board must open up decision-making power so the leaders can learn this critical thinking skill, and much of the learning is in constructive conflict. CCM needs to develop a mentor program to increase constructive conflict behavior. "Leaders use their role as mentor, and leaders use their experience to advise and give suggestions to others about how to handle specific conflict situations" (Runde & Flanagan, 2013, p.265). To enhance the mentor program, the senior leaders will be given three to four mid-level managers as their mentees. The critical piece of the mentoring program is that the "leader must be able to and willing to intervene, coach, and influence those in conflict" (p.118). For leaders in CCM, this will need increased development as it is outside the norm of the organization.

Power-distance with Board and Staff

Through the actions of the board, much of resolution has been one sided without a win-win solution. The board of CCM is not at fault because of previous leaders who acted unethically, but now it is time for CCM's board to encourage good-faith dissent in order to have constructive communication in meetings. These conversations can help grow CCM out of their current stagnation.

The board has to allow critical information to flow to the senior leadership team so they can solve the conflict problems. For example, how can global leaders be developed if they never talk to international partners and if all problems and conflict are handled at the board level only without passing the information down to the senior leadership team? For conflict competent leaders to be developed, the board has to share knowledge without fear.

Pushing responsibility down instead of up during conflict

This guideline is a huge challenge for CCM. The custom in the organization is to push conflict up to the top leaders. For an effective conflict competent leader, the senior leadership team has to teach lower and mid-level managers to address conflict in their area or region.

CCM has to find a leader to champion "the process of creating a conflict competent organization" (Runde & Flanagan, 2013, p.263). The goal of the training for the senior leadership team is to identify the champion to be the model of a conflict competent leader. After identifying the champion of the program, this senior leader will influence others to demonstrate constructive behavior. Being a champion in CCM will be a difficult assignment since he must also become a change agent as the culture in the organization will change.

Using a system to develop competence

Creating an effective system to develop conflict competence is difficult. For CCM, the challenges are great as they move from destructive to constructive behaviors in conflict. Developing an effective conflict competence system starts with a self-assessment. It is important that leaders assess what types of conflict situations trigger their destructive behaviors.

The next step is to develop team unity through a conflict agreement. The goal is to start with the senior leadership team. The team needs to develop a conflict agreement that allows for freedom to disagree to develop their constructive conflict skills.

In order for CCM to implement an effective system, the conflict competence has to start from the top. Awakening an organization to constructive behavior takes time, but it has to come from those in charge. Part of the process is for the senior leadership team to learn how to lead with integrity and correctly understand power in relationships, power-distance, and disbursement to followers.

Conclusion

As this chapter demonstrates, being a global leader with integrity is not just about managing money or keeping the letter of the law. The complexities are deeply ingrained in the operation of the organization. Although ethics plays a big part of being a leader with integrity, followers trust leaders who correctly use and control power. Understanding the use of power in relationships inside and outside of the organization is critical in effective leadership.

A global leader has to understand situational ethics in context and culture. A leader's integrity depends on how he or she will manage power in the context of power-distance and relationships in the culture. There is not a cookie-cutter approach to situational ethics. A global leader has to find his own process that depends on how he views time, ambivalence, and sense of self. Although there are too many variables to prescribe a specific step-by-step approach, in Chapter 8 I will address a few development processes for integrity.

Integrity and purpose are connected in so many ways. How can a person lead with integrity and not have a purpose for the organization? It is virtually impossible. Complexities do a great job of discouraging leaders, which can test their purpose and cause them to lose their integrity. The next chapter discusses the second principle for global leaders to manage complexities in global leadership: purpose.

4

PURPOSE

As I was spiraling into bankruptcy and watching from a hospital bed, the business that I had spent seven years building was crumbling around me, and my purpose was greatly tested. How did it come to this abrupt halt? My purpose and vision had been clear. Where did I go wrong? As most have learned in global business, success does not hinge on what you do wrong as much as on what situation you are placed into. The ambiguous environment of leading an organization in the global market requires a purpose that can be transformed to meet the current environment.

The transformation of my purpose started as a graduate student. In 1998 I made my first trip overseas to study at the Czech Management Center as part of Auburn University's MBA program. Our focus was on strategic management, and we researched the transition of the former Soviet Bloc countries into capitalist systems. We also traveled to other countries outside The Czech Republic. By visiting Hungary and Romania, I formed a deep connection with the plight of the emerging world leader. This connection was partly based on the fact that my grandparents all worked in cotton mills starting in the late 1920s until the 1980s. I saw many similarities, which developed in me a purpose to serve emerging leaders who needed so much help.

In 2002, my vision to serve emerging world leaders became a reality when I founded Sun Consulting Services, LLC. It took two years to land our first international business contract by connecting a Jordanian company with a Chinese supplier. In 2007 we opened an office in Hong Kong, which was the first step of our five year plan to open five offices around the world. My dream to be based in one of the global hubs of the emerging world was a reality. Then an earthquake, the global economic crisis, and my kidney stones hit.

Just ten years after my first overseas trip to the Czech Republic, my purpose of serving emerging world leaders had led me to bankruptcy and had taken a toll on my family, my health, my employees, and my partners. Was I to give up and not return to Hong Kong or return to Hong Kong and find a different process to fulfill my purpose?

The need was still great. Global leadership is complex for MBA grads from top universities who freely travel the world. Imagine how hard it is for a Chinese leader who grew up under the tumult of the cultural revolution, a Cambodian that experienced the horrific genocide of Khmer Rouge that took out an education system, or a Palestinian refugee who grew up outside his own country because his family was displaced. My purpose to serve these types of people was still strong, so I had to create a new funding mechanism to continue to serve the emerging world leaders.

Introduction to Purpose

By definition, a purpose is an intended or desired result, end, aim, or goal. Being from Alabama, I've observed that most people there have two main purposes – hunting and football. People in Alabama love to hunt, so they make sacrifices to purchase guns, camouflage clothes, and the many other accessories needed to kill a deer. Every person in Alabama must choose a side in the bitter Auburn/Alabama football rivalry. The desired results are bagging a 10-point buck and gloating about your team's victory to your friend whose team lost. In the same way, global leaders must have a purpose for their followers to be motivated to make the sacrifices necessary to accomplish the vision.

In order to fulfill your purpose, you need a vision, a desired outcome. As a leader if you do not have a purpose or a cause, not many people are going to follow you. And if they do follow you, you will lead them in the wrong direction. The following areas must be part of fulfilling your purpose:

1. Clear Objective - This doesn't mean that all of your life is a clear path to your objective, but your movement toward your purpose never stops. The objective of your life is clear, and this guides your decisions to the end.

2. Strategy or Plan (to reach the objective) - Once you develop the objective, you have to plan and create a strategy in order to accomplish your purpose.

3. Ability to Implement the Plan - Words, words, words are not what true leaders use the most. A leader must implement the strategy to achieve the objectives. A saying describing this process is "the proof is in the pudding." A leader backs up his or her words with actions that implement a strategy to achieve the objectives in order to live with a purpose and vision.

Failed leadership is when people who believe they are leading focus on purposes that directly benefit themselves. They want others to serve them to make their lives comfortable, easy, and noticed. Unfortunately for countless people, they go home feeling like a failure on a regular basis.

Purpose, as a principle of leadership, is about others. Yes, there are times that leaders benefit from the purpose, but the leader does not own the purpose; they share it. When the leaders try to own the purpose, the strategy usually becomes ineffective. Since I am a firm believer that leadership is not a title but an act, the act of purpose is truly an important principle in establishing yourself as a leader.

Principle #2 Purpose

Understands and clearly articulates an inspired vision of the company's goals and mission; aligns team's goals with company's goals; committed to the company's core values and culture.

The articulation depends on character and integrity as much as words. When leading across cultures, the global leader has to be very careful how the vision is communicated to ensure it is effective in reaching the target audience.

Building blocks to purpose

Before we dive into the practical ways to manage the complexities of purpose and vision, it is important to understand my premise for how a purpose is developed. An effective purpose is built around an individual worldview. What do I mean by worldview?

"An individual's worldview is the set of deeply held beliefs and fundamental assumptions which serve as a mental map for providing coherence to what the world and life are and how they work. An individual's worldview is more deeply ingrained than attitudes, opinions, traits, and values" Dent (2013).

In Dent's (2013) research to measure individuals' worldviews, he identified two types of worldviews. The first is a traditional worldview, and the second is an emerging worldview. I contend that global leaders have an emerging worldview that sees the world holistically and not as small individual parts. They also see mutual causation in their actions instead of a traditional linear causation.

From the emerging worldview, the global leader develops a global mindset. This mindset is portrayed by the leader's ability to influence groups from different backgrounds. From the global mindset the global leader is able to effectively communicate to multiple cultures in a systematic process that creates an effective purpose and strategy. In order to understand the complexities of having a purpose as a global leader, it is important to identify the culprits of the complexity.

The following chapter looks in more detail at effective communication of a global leader through strategic communication. The last section is a case study of a global leader Mohammed Yunus of Grameen Bank who had a worldview that produced a global mindset that businesses and non-profits can work together to end hunger.

How does purpose help manage complexities?

Developing a purpose with global impact requires the ability to clearly articulate your objectives and goals. It also takes creativity to enlist followers. A global leader has to inspire followers to join the purpose. This action is more than just bringing in a group of people to perform operational tasks. To enlist followers you must communicate effectively.

To inspire a vision requires that "leaders breathe life into the hopes and dreams of others and enable them to see the exciting possibilities that the future holds" (Kouzes and Posner, 2007, p.18). Global leaders have to understand and determine what is meaningful to others. The global leader has to see the purpose as collective and give followers a voice in the process of developing and implementing strategy. The key issue is for the leader to be strategic in communication in order to provide meaning and a connection to all involved. This requires the global leader to lead strategically.

Along with developing a strategic plan, the global leader has to implement the plan. This plan intertwines with the purpose and vision for the organization and can only be successful if effectively communicated. Unlike what most leaders assume, communicating is not based on telling, but instead it starts with listening.

Effective Communication

> *"To describe an **Effective Communicator,** we concentrate not on what you are saying, but how well you are listening."*

I define an effective communicator as one who speaks and writes well and practices attentive and active listening and one who has the patience to hear and can accurately restate opinions of others even when disagreeing. When it is time to speak, the effective communicator is clear and maintains two-way dialogue with others. Typically, we think of leaders standing in front of thousands giving a motivational speech. This way of leadership receives the most attention, but this is not the type of leadership that pushes organizations forward to success.

Barriers to Effective Communication

Below are four of the more common barriers to being effective in sharing a purpose/vision.

1. People are only talking to prove they are correct.
2. Instead of listening to responses of the person you are communicating with, the leader is only thinking about the next great point he or she is going to prove in the conversation.
3. A leader nods or shakes his head in agreement with the person talking but really has no idea what is being said.
4. A leader sees conversations as a debate instead of a dialogue.

The key to breaking down barriers is for the conversation to be seen as a partnership and focused on a win-win outcome instead of a competitive based conversation. For this key characteristic in sharing your purpose, you are looking for people to win in the conversation with you instead of you just proving your point.

To become a NextGen Global Leader who leads a successful organization, you must first listen and then speak. This is not debate listening in which you seek to counter-argue or exploit the point but rather an active listening that has the attitude of "How can I help the person talking?" instead of "How can I take advantage of the person talking?" This is the main distinction in becoming a NextGen Global Leader.

Once the global leader implements effective communication skills, then they have to communicate strategically. There is so much involved in strategic communication which allows the global leader to be successful. Much of the success of strategic communication is based on the global leader's ability to work as a team player.

Strategic Communication

One of the fastest ways to sabotage organizational goals and kill your purpose is by not having cognitive skills to think strategically as a leader. Strategic leaders "transform their companies to cope with globalization, increasing international competition, and more rapidly changing technology and society" (Yukl, 2010, p.368). For strategic leaders this influence is critical because it affects innovation and adaption. Part of innovation and adaption is directly related to the ability of the strategic leader to structure the organization to perform at the highest level. The structure works the best when it is based on the objective and goals of the purpose. The global leader has to speak the organization into a structure that is optimal for performance. This speaking is called strategic communication.

If communication is to make meaning, then what is strategic communication? "The term strategic communication describes the combination of plans, goals, practices and tools" (Patterson & Radtke, 2009, p.7). The problem with communication today is a person has to know which technologies can effectively influence the target audience.

Working Together

Burtis and Turman (2010) provide an effective framework for strategic communication. Their core concept states that the "power to get things done usually comes from getting other people to work well together" (p.4). How things get done in a group is centered on the leadership explaining why people should perform actions in a group. The process of leadership in a group has to take place with words, which is the critical piece of communication.

The group communicates from their exigency. This is their "compelling impulse" (p.8) to communicate to others in the group. Those who are compelled to communicate become the direction-givers in the group. These direction-givers are the people who help the groups work together effectively.

Burtis and Turman (2010) give five types of direction-givers, but they also note the direction-giver is not necessarily a title in the group but just having the ability to communicate. The five types are doer, follower, guide, manager, and leader. "A key direction-giver is someone to whom others look for guidance on a given subject, in using a particular process, or in hopes of a particular type of direction" (p.17). This role is critical during crisis situations when the group needs clear direction and clear communication.

All groups have to receive communication that provides direction. This does not necessarily have to come from one or two people, but everyone in the group is responsible. Power in leadership is ensuring everyone is involved in the group while not hoarding the communication. Anyone in the group can have an exigency, and the communication lines have to be open for the group to benefit from this communication.

Most of the time, global leaders are the direction givers in their organizations. Therefore, I am synthesizing direction-giving research with global leadership. Group dynamics are constantly changing for global leaders, so as direction-givers they must respond appropriately when others in the group communicate from their exigencies and act in an appropriate way in order to attract attention and trust. In the midst of these actions, a doer, follower, and guide must exercise skillsets in promoting credentials, demonstrating competence, and building credibility.

A vital part of a global leader's direction-giving skills is the ability to persuade others. A global leader's persuasion has three distinct traits. They are a direction-givers intentions, good sense, and good moral character. By the influence of values and character on the skillsets of direction-givers such as doers, followers, and guides, a person can determine that an effective follower makes an effective leader.

To clearly communicate the vision and goals of the group and to transform the group during crisis takes effective leadership. "People act as leaders through an ongoing interaction between crisis and the activities and orientations of those who perceive it as such" (Burtis & Turman, 2010, p.67). Perception is extremely important. The group has to perceive the communication of the leader as credible in which the leader has proven himself or herself through credentials.

A Framework to Strategic Communication

A framework should have a philosophy that promotes a person's values in action. Guidelines provide practical advice in accomplishing an effective direction-giving framework. The global leader needs to frame the purpose to persuade others to follow while building the perception of being a capable leader. Leaders build the perception through positioning and competition.

Although using the words *positioning* and *competition* in a group or team setting seems detrimental, these are both needed elements for a direction-giver to succeed. Positioning is an important because a direction-giver has to understand how to communicate the roles and responsibilities for the plan to be implemented. Positioning is how the global leader demonstrates what resources someone can offer to the purpose. The direction-giver has to position the team members in a way to gain the group's attention and interest. The currency of leadership is attention.

Positioning is critical and complex especially when the communication is usually not face-to-face. When sharing the leader's purpose and developing a strategic plan, the communication has to be planned and concise because it is usually translated and interpreted by managers and others in the different offices. To manage the human resources in diverse cultures takes a skill level unique to global leaders. To ensure the ability to communicate in this environment is to shape a story or narrative.

Shape the Story

The stories the direction-giver develops for the group are part of an ongoing story. Each new story is added to the direction-givers experience and it builds a narrative, which is a story with a plot and characters. The narrative is used in communication with the group to help the group succeed.

A direction-giver builds the narrative by making stories have an emotional appeal. From developing an emotional appeal, the others in the group are motivated to increase effectiveness, but the narrative has to connect to the group participants. To accomplish this feat, the story has to reach a master narrative. This outline version of the story is a holistic view of the situation that includes the past, present, and future. The master narrative encompasses all that is important to not only the direction-giver but the entire group.

The direction-giver communicates an effective master narrative by knowing what the group wants to hear. This takes listening skills and emotional intelligence to understand the needs of the group in order to reach them emotionally. From this connection, the master narrative builds a cohesive group.

Lessons from a Global Leader

As I described earlier, it is important for a global leader to have a purpose that develops into a vision with clear objectives and goals. Then the global leader has to implement the strategic plan. The first part of implementing the strategic plan is to effectively communicate, which starts with listening to followers to build a win-win relationship. Once a global leader uses the communication to strategically position people to accomplish the purpose and vision, the leader must turn to framing stories. One effective way of framing a story is to look for examples from leadership stories.

Theory into Practical

Although I have never met Mohammed Yunus, I am a big fan. He is one of the founders of modern social entrepreneurship. By starting Grameen Bank, he has helped thousands come out of poverty in Bangladesh. He also has been a model for countless others. Below is his story and how he worked in a global team (partnership) with a multi-national company to fulfill his purpose of ending poverty in Bangladesh. He does a great job in framing through positioning in this case study.

Muhammed Yunnus: Power of Framing Your Story

* All quotes from "Creating a World Without Poverty" (2007) by Muhammad Yunus

In his book *Creating a World Without Poverty*, Muhammed Yunus, or Professor Yunus as some call him, demonstrates his spiritual intelligence and leadership ability through his purpose:

> I believe in free markets as sources of inspiration and freedom for all, not as architects of decadence for small elite. The world's richest countries, in North America,

Europe, and parts of Asia have benefited enormously from the creative energies, efficiencies, and dynamism that free markets produce. I have devoted my life to bringing those same benefits to the world's most neglected people- the very poor, who are not factored in when economists and business people speak about the market.

Professor Yunus used his experience of living among the poor and teaching at a university in the U.S. to develop a task:

My experience has shown me that the free market-- powerful and useful as it is -- could address the problems like global poverty and environmental degradation, but not if it must cater solely and relentlessly to the financial goals of its richest shareholders. To make sure the structure of capitalism complete, we need to introduce another kind of business one that recognizes the multidimensional nature of human beings. If we described our existing companies as profit maximizing businesses, the new kind of business might be called social business.

In that description, you can see his ability to mix compassion for the poor with cognitive decisions such as a strategy for a social business. So how does this social business operate? "A social business is a company that is cause driven rather than profit driven with the potential to act as a change agent for the world."

Professor Yunus uses sensemaking to develop a strategy. Another strength is his ability to exhibit self-awareness and self-management from a high emotional intelligence through partnering with a global team of leaders. The final part is the effectiveness of positioning.

Strategy for Change

One of the frameworks of sensemaking is commitment. Professor Yunus was able to combine his purpose of alleviating poverty with a clear strategy.

Below are a few examples that illustrate his commitment and identity in sensemaking:

1. A social business that manufactures and sells high quality, nutritious food products at very low prices to a targeted market of poor and underfed children. These products can be cheaper because they do not compete in the luxury market and therefore don't require costly packaging or advertising because the company that sells them is not compelled to maximize its profits.

2. A social business that designs and markets health insurance policies to provide affordable medical care to the poor.

3. A social business that develops renewable energy systems and sells them at reasonable prices to rural communities that otherwise can't afford access to energy.

4. A social business that recycles garbage, sewage, and other waste products that would otherwise generate pollution in poor or politically powerless neighborhoods.

The next step is seeing how Professor Yunus brings his strategy into reality through a global network.

The Global Team

Professor Yunus tells how his vision became a reality at an unexpected time while he was traveling to France. A few days before his trip, his travel coordinator in Paris received a message from the office of Frank Riboud, the chairman and CEO of Danone Group, a large French Corporation. The message read: "Mr. Riboud has heard about the work of Professor Yunus in Bangladesh, and he would like very much like to meet him. Since you will be traveling to Deauville shortly, would it be possible for him to have lunch with Mr. Riboud in Paris."

Professor Yunus immediately opened up the conversation with his purpose. "I am always happy to meet with people interested in my work in general, and a microcredit in particular, especially if they can help in the battle to alleviate and totally eliminate global poverty." Then Professor Yunus described the strengths of Grameen Bank. One of its most successful ventures had "developed a series of businesses, some operated on profit-making basis, some as nonprofits that were improving economic opportunities for the poor and many other ways. They range from bringing telephone and Internet communication services to thousands of remote villages to helping traditional weavers bring their products to market." The example gave a good foundation for the conversation and showed Professor Yunus' ability to be self-aware in the situation. He was not intimidated but shared his vision with the CEO of a multi-billion dollar company.

Once Professor Yunus completed his explanation of Grameen Bank, he wanted to listen to why Mr. Riboud wanted to meet him for lunch, especially since Group Danone did not operate in Bangledesh. After hearing about Group Danone, Professor Yunus was still confused on why he was invited to lunch. Mr. Riboud was ready with an answer:

> Danone is an important source of food in many regions of the world. That includes some of the developing nations where hunger is a serious problem. We have a major business in Brazil, and Indonesia, and in China. Recently we have expanded into India. In fact, more than 40% of our business is in developing markets. We don't want to sell our products only to the well-off people in those countries. We would like to find ways to help feed the poor. It is part of our company's historic commitment to be socially innovative and progressive, which dates back 35 years to the work of my father, Antoine Riboud.

Professor Yunus' ability to self-manage by innovation and creativity had created a reputation. Mr. Riboud heard of this reputation and "thought that a man and an organization that had used creative thinking to help so many of the poor might have an idea or two for Group Danone." Professor Yunus was still confused and did not understand exactly why Mr. Riboud was telling him this information, so Riboud continued:

> I've been thinking a lot about the role of business in helping the world's poor. Other economic sectors-- the volunteer, charitable, and nongovernmental sectors, for

instance-- devote a great deal of time and energy to dealing with poverty and its consequences. But business-- the most financially innovative and efficient sector of all--has no direct mechanism to apply its practices to the goal of eliminating poverty.

During this part of the conversation, Professor Yunus' emotional intelligence peaked, and he had a thought. "It was a spur of the moment impulse, not the carefully planned business proposal that most executives prefer. But over the years, I've found that some of my best projects have been started, not on the basis of rigorous prior analysis and planning, but simply from the impulse that says, 'Here is a chance to do something good.'"

Then, Professor Yunus dreamed out loud and brought together a plan:

> As you know the people of Bangladesh are some of the poorest in the world. Malnutrition is a terrible problem, especially among children. It leads to awful health consequences as the children grow up. Your company is a leading producer of nutritious foods. What would you think about creating a joint venture to bring some of your products to the villages of Bangladesh? We would create a company that we own together and call it Grameen Danone. It could manufacture healthful foods that will improve the diet of rural Bangladeshis-- especially the children. If the products were sold at a low price, we could make a real difference in the lives of millions of people.

Professor Yunus thought to himself, "I was about to learn that Mr. Riboud, CEO of one of the world's best-known companies, could be just as impulsive as a banker to the poor of Bangladesh." Mr. Riboud rose and extended his hand. "Let's do it," Mr. Riboud said, and they shook hands. But there was one more part of the sensemaking that needed to be explained.

Professor Yunus added a last proposal to the plan. "I am not done with my proposal yet. Our joint venture will be a social business." Mr. Riboud said, "A social business? What is that?" Professor Yunus replied,

"It's a business designed to meet a social goal. In this case, the goal is to improve the nutrition of poor families in the villages of Bangladesh. A social business is a business that pays no dividends. It sells products at prices that make it self-sustaining. The owners of this company can get back the amount they've invested in the company over a period of time, but no profit is paid to investors in the form of dividends. Instead, any profit made stays in the business to finance expansion, to create new products and services, and to do more good for the world."

Mr. Riboud responded, "This is extremely interesting. Let's do it." From this agreement, Group Danone and Grameen worked as a global team to create a new model- a multinational social business.

Leadership Effectiveness:

Since publishing this book, Grameen Danone has already experienced success with the multinational social business:

1. First plant in Bogra is in full operation.
2. Around 400 small milk producers and 250 "Grameen ladies" have been employed to supply the raw materials for the yogurt and to sell the product in the surrounding villages.
3. Forecast showed a long-term appeal for children in the rural area so already have plans to break ground on building a second yogurt plant.
4. "Ultimately our dream of a network of up to 50 such plants around Bangladesh remains achievable."

5

SACRIFICE

The transformation of my purpose and vision started in the fall of 2008 while I sat in the Sanatorium Hospital in Hong Kong. I was rushed to the hospital in extreme pain as a large kidney stone tried to fit through a small space. I sat for a few days waiting for the lithotripsy machine to have an opening (it seems many people in Hong Kong have kidney stones), so I had plenty of time to think. My wife was 45 minutes away by train, and she was having problems with her pregnancy, so most of my stay in the hospital was alone, unless you count the seven Chinese patients sharing my room.

Visitors to the hospital were amazed at the *gweilo* (foreigner) in the bed, so at times I would have a visitor peek in though the curtains to stare, smile, and laugh. After a few shots of morphine, I started playing along with the curious visitors. I was trying my best not to allow the reality of the situation to set in. I was living in a foreign country and stuck at a local hospital with foreign doctors. All of this at a critical time in the company when I did not need to be out of the office.

As the days passed, the more frustration sat in, and I really needed to do some soul searching since I couldn't do much except stare at a computer. I kept asking myself the question, "Are you happy?" I wasn't asking if I was a happy person, but was I happy in fulfilling my purpose through Sun Consulting Services? I really enjoyed serving emerging world leaders in their leadership development process, but the stress of charging these companies fees for the services, marketing my company to new projects, managing two offices, and managing projects in five continents caused me to have an overload.

The company eventually failed, but before that happened I realized how to transform to meet my purpose. It was to find another funding mechanism for serving emerging world leaders. The new funding mechanism would take a great sacrifice to learn another industry - nonprofits. In the end, it was about sacrificing a lifestyle to reach my purpose. Was I willing to let go of being Jay Clark, the international business owner, to reframe my story and achieve the ultimate purpose?

This action was going to take self-sacrifice and also affect my family and the people in my organization. As I returned to Hong Kong in early 2009, I was determined to implement the transformation. My wife and I started Kerusso Foundation, Inc., a U.S. 501 c3 charitable organization. This allowed us to raise funds to serve emerging world leaders. Initially, funds were limited, so I continued to work independently on a few consulting projects. This transition taught me that my purpose and vision were clear. I was not dedicated to building a large company, but my true passion and purpose was serving the emerging global leader.

So what type of sacrifice?

When one thinks of sacrifice, it is usually in extremes like someone dying or giving up basic rights. Although global leaders are sometimes faced with these extreme measures when accomplishing their purpose, the type of sacrifice described in this principle is more practical to everyday life.

The notion of an 8 to 5 job for a global leader is long past. So one of the first sacrifices a global leader has to make is adjusting the schedule to the followers. This could mean early morning or late night conference calls, which expands the hours the global leader needs to work and makes the work/life balance much more difficult.

Below is a list of the primary areas where a global leader has to sacrifice. This is not an exhaustive list, but it covers the general areas. The global leader sacrifices both individually and relationally. The leader's family must make sacrifices, and the people the global leader serves have to sacrifice.

Principle #3 Sacrifice

A leader will see sacrifices in three primary areas.

1. *Individual- Being a leader means you sacrifice individually for your purpose to be achieved. Many times there is a financial sacrifice to start on the path of obtaining your purpose, but the most demanding is sacrificing your local identity for a global identity.*
2. *Family- In leadership you constantly have to ask your family to sacrifice, and that is why they have to believe in your cause just as much as you do. In four years, my wife and increasing number of children have moved across the Pacific four times.*
3. *Those you serve- As a leader it seems that everyone wants a piece of your attention and time, so even the people you serve will need to sacrifice and allow you to grow as a leader.*

The demands of travel alone are enough to challenge the sacrificial ability of any global leader and his or her family. But one of the greatest challenges for a global leader is sacrificing a local identity to gain global followers.

How does sacrifice manage the complexity of global leadership?

When discussing sacrifice and global leadership, the first place to start is leading self. To manage the complexities of global leadership, the leader is challenged by self-motivation to adapt in a life of ambiguities. Self-leadership also incorporates the sacrifice of the family as they are moved around the world to fulfill the vision. Humility of the global leader is the last part of sacrifice that manages complexity in global leadership. This is not just personal humility but also organizational humility.

Self-Leadership

The problem of researching the topic of leading self is the broad scope of definitions for leadership. The process of synthesizing published works in the political, organizational, and academic realms comes first in identifying the principles of leading self. The definition of self-leadership is "managing one's own thoughts and behaviors in order to intrinsically pursue goals effectively and be productive" (Furtner, Rauthmann, & Sachse, 2010, p. 1191). Four distinct areas of behavior describe self-leadership. They are character, self-actualization, self-awareness, and self-empowerment.

The first behavioral tendency of leading self is character. "Character strengths can be defined as positive traits reflected in thoughts, feelings, and behaviors" (Park, Peterson, & Seligman, 2004, p. 603). These character strengths increase judgment and lead to human excellence. Character strengths are distinguished from talents and abilities as they are strengths that a person can reflect upon and talk to others about. Furtner et al. writes that self-leadership consists of three strategic dimensions. The first strategic dimension is behavior-focused such as goal setting, self-reward, self-observation. A second strategic dimension is natural reward strategies such as intrinsic motivation. A self-leader shows the third strategic dimension with constructive thought patterns. These constructive thought patterns evaluate beliefs and assumptions.

Burns connects Maslow's work on self-actualization to a leader's success. Self-actualization is to Maslow a complex class of 'higher' needs, less imperative than that for sheer survival, less related to brute physical and psychological needs, a need more healthy psychologically, tending toward more creativity and a better balance between individual and collective claims, a continuing striving for efficacy in a series of challenges and tasks. It represents motivation to become those positive qualities that are a potential growth of the self (Burns, 1978, p. 116).

Through self-actualization leaders gain flexibility, the ability to assess personal needs of others, and an open-mindedness, which leads to successful leadership. In self-actualization, the leader leads others most effectively through leading self. The activity of leadership requires leaders to possess the skill to "perceive needs of followers in relationship to their own, to help followers move toward fuller self-realization and self-actualization along with the leaders themselves" (Burns, 1978, p.116). Going past the technical definition of Maslow, Burns expands self-actualization in that leaders have to increase their capacity to learn from others and the environment.

Leaders need the capacity of self-actualization that allows them to listen, be guided by others, and not be threatened by them.

"From self-awareness - understanding one's emotions and being clear about one's purpose - flows self-management, the focused drive that all leaders need to achieve their goals" (Goleman, Boyatzis, & McKee, 2002, p. 45). When leaders have control over emotions and self-management, they are more adaptable to changing environments and can overcome obstacles. Another important trait of a self-managed leader is transparency, which provides trustworthiness, honesty, and integrity.

A leader's social cognitive ability is to influence self. Through self-influence, the leader produces the self-motivation to learn, communicate, and develop adaptive strategies. These skills are predicated on the behavior or social cognitive ability of the person to self-regulate. "Although special problems such as managing time or controlling stress have received specific attention, managing one's day-to-day behavior has been largely neglected" (Neck & Manz, 2013, p. 113).

By following these self-leadership behaviors, a global leader will increase in effectiveness to lead because the complexities will become more manageable. The challenges of global leadership require leaders to sacrifice individual freedoms by moving to countries not like their own. Their families have to sacrifice due to the huge struggles of living as a family overseas.

The next step in being a sacrificial leader is having humility in an organization. The global leader sacrifices to create a culture of humility. The type of humility that is needed is described next.

Humility

In a world that is suffering under a crisis in leadership, one can point to answering the question of humility as an important factor in solving this crisis. Yet the people on the cover of business books in the local bookstore do not fit the perceived definition of humility. The word *humility* conjures up many different images, and most are negative, such as a monk or a lowly servant. Because of humility's connection to religion, describing a leader as humble can bring negative feelings. For many leaders, the last word they would use to describe themselves is humble. One of the main reasons is the lack of knowledge of the definition of humility, traits of humility, and how humility makes a leader more effective.

As researchers dissect humility in greater detail, certain traits of humility are useful for leaders today. A few researchers are starting to point to humility as the answer to the crisis by describing that "true leadership—the essence of what people long for and want desperately to follow—implies a certain humility that is appropriate and elicits the best response from people" (Blanchard, 2007, p. 268). The importance of humility is not just for individuals, but it also permeates into organizations. The complexity of the global market drives the need for humble leaders. If global leaders do not know the complex realities of their environment, they struggle with direction-giving. For this reason "leaders need to seek, offer, provide, and accept help" (Schein, 2011, p.4). To meet the complexity of today's organizations, a leader has to set a foundation of humility, which allows servility and authenticity to thrive.

Defining Humility

The challenge of defining humility is separating the religious tones of humility from a virtue that is measurable in organizations. The measurement will not only pertain to individual leaders but for the entire organization. To define humility a framework is created through a synopsis of contextual meanings of humility. Intellectual and organizational humility are the two most prevalent areas in the various definitions. From these two contexts, a foundational definition can be found which is imperative to discovering if the development of humility is possible.

Intellectual Humility

What is intellectual humility? "Intellectual humility is a very low concern for intellectual domination in the form of leaving the stamp of one's mind on disciples, one's field, and future intellectual generations" (Roberts & Wood, 2007, p. 250). This type of humility has a concern for knowledge, especially the attributes of truth, justice, precision, and significance. Roberts and Wood build the definition of intellectual humility by contrasting with its antonyms vanity, arrogance, and hubris.

One of the most referenced philosophers on intellectual humility is Immanuel Kant. Even though most of his work in the *Critique of Practical Reason (1952)* was writing against the Christian interpretation of humility, Kant still provided enough material to develop a following on the topic of humility. Kant saw that "all the moral perfection that a human being can attain is still only virtue, … a self-esteem combined with humility" (Kant, 1952, p. 346). Kant combined humility with self-esteem, but instead of using servility like the religious definition of humility, Kant inserted a true noble pride. Kant and fellow philosopher Hume saw servility as a monkish humility.

The challenge with Kant's intellectual humility is the infusion of self-esteem. Can a leader be humble when dealing with the dialectic challenge of self-esteem, which involves a measure of pride? Louden interprets that Kant thinks Christian humility "forfeits the proper self-esteem that is necessary for moral agency" (Louden, 2007, p. 634). For this reason, Kant writes more about moral humility. Although Kant places moral strength and courage above humility, he still considers humility to be a virtue. With this type of self-esteem, a leader "does not think too highly of self" and gives "proper credit to others where credit is due" (Solomon, 1999, p. 93). Another way to describe humility is that it lies somewhere between arrogance and a lack of self-esteem.

In contrast to Kant's intellectual humility, Roberts and Wood (2007) do categorize humility as a virtue. It is a virtue because the acquisition, maintenance, transmission, and application of knowledge are integral parts of human life, and a life characterized by humility with respect to these activities, as well as many other activities, is a more excellent life than one that lacks it.

From the foundation of Aristotelian ethics and moving through the ages, epistemology has seen changes. Roberts and Wood surmised the best framework for intellectual virtues is to return to 17th century epistemology. One reason for taking this approach is to avoid the deconstruction of epistemology by the postmodern philosophers, which takes away the ability to learn intellectual virtues. The problem is only a minority of people try to seek intellectual virtues through propositional knowledge. There are two features of propositional knowledge.

The first is that it is knowledge of a relatively isolated proposition. The proposition is true, and the subject holds it in an attitude of believing and is warranted in holding it with that attitude. The second feature is that, for any proposition, you either know it or you don't; this kind of knowledge does not come in degrees. (Roberts & Wood, 2007, p. 43)

By following Roberts and Wood rationalization of intellectual humility and propositional knowledge, it is a key component to determining the possibility of humility development for organizational leaders.

Organizational Humility

To this point, the focus has been on the aspect of humility for an individual. To accomplish the goal of building a framework of humility in organizations, the organization itself needs to develop humility collectively. Solomon (1999) makes a connection between an individual's and an organization's need for virtues. In this philosophical view, if an individual needs the virtue of humility, then it is a natural progression to say that an organization also needs virtues.

Hubris is the opposite of humility, so organizations led by leaders with hubris are less humble organizations. Jim Collins defines the concept of hubris as "excessive pride that brings down a hero, or alternatively, outrageous arrogance that inflicts the suffering upon the innocent" (p.29). He gives an example of an organization with hubris, Motorola, that laid off 60,000 employees in two years. From Collins' research, he provided the five stages of decline that lead to the failure of an organization. Hubris born of success sets the foundation in which the arrogance of organizations is the first stage of decline. An undisciplined pursuit of more, a denial of risk and peril, and a grasping for salvation are attitudes of hubris that cause organizations to make bad decisions.

If hubris causes an organization to make arrogant decisions leading to its decline, how does one define a humble organization? Virtues are dynamic in nature and "capable of improvement or deterioration" (Vera & Rodriguez-Lopez, 2004, p. 394), so defining a humble organization starts with a foundation in business ethics described by Aristotle. Solomon (1999) paraphrases Aristotle's approach to business ethics:

> It was Aristotle who insisted on the virtues, or "excellences," as the basic constituents of individual and collective happiness. The underlying assumption was that a person is who he or she is by virtue of the community, in turn, nurture and encourage each of its members to be a good person (Solomon, 1999, p.xxiv).

By using Solomon's description of Aristotelian business ethics, a definition of a humble organization is clearer. For Aristotle the people and community were connected; therefore, the actions of the community provided the virtues of the people in the community. One can determine that if an organization has hubris then the leaders in the organization will too. If an organization is humble, then the leaders in the organization are leading with humility.

Crossan, Vera, and Nanjad (2008) describe transcendent leadership as a strategic leader who leads self, others, and the organization. The 8th proposition of the paper states that "the transcendent leader, who has high levels of leadership of self, others, and organization, will be associated with the highest level of firm performance" (Crossan, Vera, & Nanjad, 2008, p. 578). The organizational leader is successful by learning how to lead in changing external environments, developing new strategies, and leading change in the organization.

From the three sections of spiritual humility, intellectual humility, and organizational humility, a definition of humility can possibly be constructed. The first part is that humility is a virtue closely related to the ability to live a virtuous life. A humble person looks for something larger than himself or herself as a guide. The second part is that humility does not center on a monkish view of humility. There is an aspect of strength involved. The third part is that an organization directly connects its actions to the people inside the organization (Solomon, 1999). If the leaders are humble, then the organization will become humble.

Traits of a Humble Leader

"Practicing simple humble behaviors makes good leaders into great leaders" (Hayes & Comer, 2011, p. 13). The realization of humble leaders helping make organizations effective became more popular with the description of the Level 5 Leader by Jim Collins. Limited empirical research on humility in the area of organizational leadership increases the importance of determining a construct of humility by listing the traits of a humble leader.

By synthesizing writings on the traits of humility, a theme of traits appears. Here is a list of abilities of a humble organizational leader: (1)to understand complexities of the organization, (2)to ask the right questions, (3)to connect to others around them, (4)to be open and authentic, and (5) to follow a greater call. By synthesizing these traits, a construct of humility is easier to design.

Ability to Understand

According to Schein (2011), organizations have become too complex to rely on one leader with hubris. In describing leadership in future organizations, "leadership will involve a constant shifting of roles as the task demands change" (Schein, 2011, p.4). To adapt to these changes, leaders have to understand the organization is complex, and therefore, they have to continuously learn. Part of this learning process is to know what role a humble leader can take to help a situation. Schein (2011) names this type of humble leader a process consultant. The team members work together to identify and solve problems that are beyond their expertise and the leader consults along the way.

An arrogant leader views success independently from the success of an organization. While a humble leader sees success tied to the organization. A similar case in sports is when a quarterback has an above-average statistical performance while the team has lost most of their games. If the quarterback says he has had a great year, he does not understand the complexities in an organization and exhibits a vice of arrogance. He lacks the knowledge that a losing team does not attract as many followers and endorsements, which will eventually mean the quarterback misses future salary.

Connection to Followers

With the synergies established between virtues and intellectual humility, being humble relates to the connection to humanity. Hayes and Comer describe this type of humility as being able to "see the importance of other's ideas, stop, and listen to them" (p.13). Each day the leader demonstrates humanness by sharing triumphs and barriers like everyone else. In other words, the leader refuses the VIP treatment and looks to be just one person in the group.

Collins explains this trait as personal humility. The top leaders, Level 5, showed an ability to "channel their ego needs away from themselves and into the larger goal of building a great company" (p.21). Collins developed the formula that *humility* plus *will* equals a Level 5 leader. The concept of being humble helps the follower see the true personality of the leader.

Open and Authentic

Being open and authentic are foundational for a leader to develop humility. The reason these traits are important is the connection to and similarity with authentic leadership. Authenticity, at times, can be interpreted as low self-esteem for the leader, but Morris shows in their research that low self-esteem is actually associated with lower levels of humility. To be open and authentic does not require a person to lose confidence. The opposite is true whereas humble leaders practicing open and authentic traits "have no need to prove anything by telling people how good they are" (Hayes & Comer, 2011, p.13).

From authentic leadership also comes another benefit. "Authentic leaders are likely to be supportive of their followers by being fair in dealings with followers, continually emphasizing the growth of followers, and considering the needs of others before their own" (Morris et al., 2005, p. 1341). The research by Morris et al. (2005) found that leader humility is a prediction to supportiveness toward others. Oddly, this research showed that humble leaders are more likely to show egalitarian actions in communicating to others. With more engaged and supportive followers, the open and authentic leaders increase their effectiveness.

Follows a Greater Call

The last trait is the most important for the success of an organizational leader. Humble leaders not only have to understand the complexities of the organization, ask the right questions, connect to others around them, and lead openly and authentically, but humble leaders also have to focus on something greater than self (Morris et al., 2005). As demonstrated earlier, Christianity and other monotheistic religions such as Judaism and Islam teach humility because there is a God. The trait of a humble leader can include religious humility, but even without religion, there is potential transcendence. In the attempt to develop humble leaders, a person has to see the organizational transcendence. There is something bigger than one leader or even one group of leaders. "People with humility don't deny their power; they just recognize that it passes through them, not from them" (Blanchard, 2007, p. 269)

Conclusion

As a global leader sacrifices, he or she is better able to manage the complexities in a challenging environment. Part of the sacrifice is self-leadership and humility. By exhibiting these traits, a global leader can make the sacrifices needed to be an effective leader. The sacrifices are not just by the leader, but also by the family and organization.

Next is a case study that describes the sacrificial leadership needed by the global leader to manage complexities. Although the names are fictitious, this is a real story of a global leader brought from the horrors of genocide to leading an organization that is helping hundreds of thousands have a chance to increase their standard of living.

LESSONS FROM A GLOBAL LEADER

Sarath's birth certificate shows he was born on August 4, 1974, but his family does not believe the birth certificate is correct. Sarath believes his real birthday is in 1971. The reason for this discrepancy is that during Sarath's birth, Cambodia was caught in the middle of the U.S. - Vietnam conflict that produced one of the harshest dictators in history, Pol Pot. When Sarath was around three years old, the Pol Pot regime began. This time period in Cambodia is referred to as the Khmer Rouge. Sarath's family, along with millions of others, were led out of Phnom Pen, the capital of Cambodia, and sent to a rural province. During the horrors of the Khmer Rouge period, Sarath was taken from his family and sent to a child labor camp.

For most people, growing up during the reign of the Khmer Rouge would destroy hope, but for Sarath it was during these years he started developing his work ethic that has been beneficial in his leadership ability. As a young child, he would have to work in the field in the morning and go to school in the afternoon. After the Khmer Rouge fled the country in 1979, the educational resources in Sarath's farming community were minimal, so his father sent him back to Phnom Penh. Since his family could not afford private tutors to help with the university entrance exam, Sarath sat outside on his bicycle under the windows of private classes to learn mathematics.

From his determination to learn and succeed, Sarath was admitted into the university and completed his Bachelor of Mathematics and a master's degree. His skills in mathematics led him into the financial services industry, and he joined Microloan, Inc. in 1999. Microloan, Inc. exists to provide sustainable financial services to Cambodia's poor entrepreneurs.

Sarath's managerial and leadership potential was recognized immediately, and he skyrocketed up the organizational ladder at Microloan, Inc. He became branch manager in Phnom Penh in 2003, was appointed operations manager in 2005, and became the first local general manager of in 2008. Under his leadership, Microloan, Inc. achieved self-sustainability and has since enabled its clients to achieve socio-economic transformation. As of March 2011, Microloan, Inc. is serving 50,452 active borrowers with outstanding loans of $34.92 million. To maximize the impact on clients, Microloan, Inc. is working with relief and development partners to provide other complementary services to clients such as debt management, savings, and budgeting.

Sacrifice and Self Leadership

When describing Sarath as a leader, the most important aspect is to view his leadership in the context of his culture. Research projects have tried to provide a connection with leadership and culture, but there is still a need for more research to adequately study the connection. The difficulty in learning about a leader in a different culture is lack of information. For example, Sarath has never had the opportunity to take assessments to gain understanding of his personality, skills, or styles.

To build a description of Sarath's leadership, it is important to produce a wide variety of understanding to achieve the goal of narrowing in on a few areas that describe Sarath's success as a leader. We used Northouse's (2010) assessments for style and skills to develop a high level of understanding of Sarath's leadership. When Sarath was assessed to determine his leadership skills, his highest score was in technical skills. With Sarath's background in finance and mathematics, it was not a surprise that he is categorized as a technical skilled leader.

From the leadership style assessment, Sarath was categorized as a relational leader. Sarath falling into this category coincides with the fact that his culture is a highly relational one. This was proven when Sarath's score was compared to the style assessment scores of 30 top leaders in Microloan, Inc. Twenty-four out of 30 leaders scored the highest in relational style.

To provide more background on Sarath's personality, the researcher matched potential personalities from the Uniquely You DISC Personality Profiles. Sarath persistently demonstrates the personality of a steady-doer. He is the type of personality that gets the job done. He prefers "stable surroundings and is determined to accomplish tasks. As a quiet leader, he relates best to small groups. He does not like to talk in front of large crowds but wants to control them. He enjoys secure relationships but often dominates them. He can be soft and hard at the same time. He is motivated by sincere challenges that allow him to systematically do great things. He prefers sure things rather than shallow recognition. He makes good friends while driving to succeed" (Carbonell & Ponz, 2006, p.15).

To pinpoint why Sarath is an effective leader, it is important to understand that through various challenges, Sarath did not become a bitter person. Instead, Sarath grew into a leader who holds the value of hard work with an understanding he can make a difference in the world. In Cambodian society, fatalistic attitudes prevail, so Sarath has overcome not only his life challenges but also many social challenges as well. He is not relying on a fatalist attitude about change, but he is a principle-centered leader who continues training, listening, and learning. Because of Sarath's growth as a principle-centered leader, it is easy to see the connection between the effectiveness of the organization and the individual.

The apex of his success is illustrated when he was named operational manager in 2003. When Sarath's operation management team began, Microloan, Inc. had a portfolio of around $600,000 in loans. Under his leadership, the organization witnessed an unprecedented growth from being a little known micro-finance institution in Cambodia to becoming one of the top five largest. While Sarath was leading the operations team, they reached over $2,000,000 in loans. This is incredible considering most loans are around $50-$100. Sarath's teamwork and leadership allowed thousands of Cambodians to receive loans to start businesses that would improve their living conditions. Sarath's leadership ability to make a better society for Cambodians was seen in his sacrifice during this time.

Foundations of Sarath's Leadership

In Sarath's development into a sacrificial leader, two primary areas influenced his ability to become an effective leader for the betterment of society. The first is the social structure or psychodynamic approach to leadership that gave Sarath his work ethic by having a strong relationship with his father. The second is his ability to adapt to a changing culture to develop as a leader.

To describe Sarath as a sacrificial leader, one needs to first understand social structures that provided him the opportunity to reach this level of leadership. The beginning of his leadership ability comes from the idea that parents help children see their purpose. The group theory of social psychology provides support to the idea that the family or social structure is crucial in the development of a leader. Leadership theorists also term this the psychodynamic approach. In the psychodynamic approach, the family of origin is an extremely important aspect of Sarath developing as a leader.

The example of the social structures influencing Sarath's leadership is his father's sacrifice to push Sarath to become a student and then a life learner. When asked questions about his father, Sarath is instantly a burst of energy. The respect that Sarath holds for his father is as vibrant today as when he was younger.

Sarath's father was the one who pushed for education, but during the first few years of the Khmer Rouge when Sarath's family was forced to leave their life in Phnom Pen, it was his mother that provided the ability to survive. His mother came from a farming family so when they arrived to their new plot of land in the village, it was his mother who had to teach the family how to grow crops in order to survive. For Sarath to leave his work in the village to travel to Phnom Pen for his education was a sacrifice for everyone in the family.

The next aspect of maturing as a leader is the courage Sarath exhibited to endure hardships such as a child labor camp and having to leave his family at an early age. By having a strong family of origin and having the ability to endure extreme circumstances, Sarath demonstrated the effectiveness of courage in the development of an effective leader. The center of this courage is his humility.

To grasp the amount of courage it took Sarath to become a leader in Cambodia, a person has to understand the background of the culture. When Sarath was ten years old, he was sent to a labor camp. As Sarath was trying to pass from childhood to young adulthood, his country was taken over by Vietnam. As Sarath was starting university and growing in his values, the United Nations essentially took over the country, and Cambodians for the first time in 20 years started experiencing, what Americans label as, freedom. What makes Sarath an effective leader is even though he lost supposed freedoms in labor camps and lost human rights taken by tyrannical dictators and foreign rulers, he never lost his freedom of self. It was Sarath's courage that gave him the ability to take responsibility in his choices while not blaming others for his circumstances.

The second area that influenced Sarath to become sacrificial in his leadership was the ability to adapt to extreme situations. Sarath had to navigate major changes that took adaptive skills. The first change was in the Cambodian society as the country went from one of the poorest in the world to a developing country over night as the investments from China,

Korea, and Japan started flooding the country. "Cambodia grew very rapidly over the last decade; GDP grew 9.1 percent per year during 1998–2008" (CDRI, 2010, p.6). The second was the adaptive challenge in leading a financial service firm in the midst of constant change. Sarath had to navigate Microloan, Inc. through many changes starting with the increase in regulations to the need to build partnerships to remain competitive with loans. Since the Cambodian banking industry was rebuilt from scratch, there were many major changes in the industry over the last 20 years. Sarath had to adapt to these challenges by keeping Microloan, Inc. competitive with loans to clients and building partnerships with foreign capital investors so Microloan, Inc. could continue to sustain growth. Keeping the equilibrium of regulations and capital takes an adaptive leader because the stress is continuous, and solutions have to come quickly.

To lead Microloan, Inc. through this turmoil of change, Sarath could not utilize the cultural view of leadership in which one person stands above all. Instead, he understood that he needed a team of leaders that would serve each other. The challenge is to produce teams that built long-term trusting relationships. This high-trust group must include members who are open about feelings, experience better communication about problems and goals, search for alternative solutions, are motivated to high performance, and will grow as a team. In the senior leadership team, Sarath was successful in achieving all of these factors of a high-trust group.

When Sarath achieved success in leading Microloan, Inc. to triple-digit growth as operations manager, he inspired his team in their work and motivated them to action. Amidst the success, Sarath's most pressing problem was the branch staff's inability to properly assess loans to minimize defaults. He needed his staff to become more efficient so they could raise more capital to provide more loans. To accomplish this goal, he worked closely with the staff to provide support through inspiring and motivating the team. With any change process, Sarath had to create a buy-in to the change, and this is when inspired motivation is essential in sacrificial leadership. The changes to policy and procedures increased the burden on his leadership because it made the staff's work more difficult. The key to his success was that the staff viewed Sarath as a teammate who worked closely with them, listening to their concerns. By this action, the staff increased performance, and the organization started growing much faster.

Sarath's strength is in this area of sacrificial leadership. I have studied Cambodian leaders for many years, and Sarath is abnormally sensitive to the opinions of and solutions from his team, specifically for each individual on the team. Sarath exemplified this characteristic when he gathered information from the field to support the branches in assessing loans in order to lower default rates.

In answering the question on this topic, Sarath gave the following reply:

> I gather the information through the field visit, sometimes just check the documents, ask the staff about flow of work, meet them, ask some questions about products, completion, leadership and management at the place, their feeling about Microloan, Inc., meet clients, also through branch reports (just read some reports not all), audit reports and the executive committee meeting and senior management meeting and also through refreshment training. Some time I take time to meet and want to hear from staff when they come for refreshment and other training at Head Office.

In this response he mentioned the words *ask* or *listen* four times. Sarath has an innate sense to use individualized consideration in his leadership. The fact that Sarath has not attended western style leadership seminars to know these terms shows that individualized consideration could possibly be connected to a person with a relational leadership style.

Conclusion

Sarath is a great example of a sacrificial leader in an effective organization. The influence of his family, specifically his father, the work ethic evolved through harsh situations, technical skills in mathematics and finance, and his relational style of leadership all come together to make him a sacrificial leader. Combining his leadership abilities with an organization like Microloan, Inc. exemplifies how a sacrificial leader influences tens of thousands to make a better society for Cambodians.

Sarath models for other global leaders that they can overcome the worst situations and still serve others. These situations posed many complex issues, but Sarath's ability to sacrifice helped manage the complexities. Through the power of effective self-leadership and humility, a global leader can influence their communities and world even with many odds against success.

As I have described the principle of sacrifice to global leaders. The next step is discipline. Even if a leader has integrity, purpose, and sacrifice, it is hard to be effective in implanting the many changes in life without discipline.

6

DISCIPLINE

This fourth principle of discipline is the "rubber-meets-the-road" characteristic. A global leader needs integrity, purpose, and sacrifice, but the critical piece is the principle of discipline. In 2009 my position required major changes as I shifted from for-profit industry to non-profit industry. Then after settling into a new routine in late 2009, my oldest daughter was diagnosed with Leukemia in early 2010.

This event shook our family, and being in Hong Kong was an added stress. We had to make decisions in a different culture, in multiple languages, and with differing views on how to treat my daughter's cancer. In the end, we had to make the hard decision to return to the United States. Little did we know that we would be back in the U.S. for five years for my daughter's cancer treatment protocol. I would make the same decision again, but it was a sacrificial decision. The move pushed me farther away from the people I served, from my purpose. Traveling back and forth from the U.S. over the last five years has given me perpetual jet lag and has challenged me in every way. It has limited my ability to expand to new countries and has filled me with anxiety during every trip worrying about my daughter.

In the midst of these struggles, I saw an opportunity. I kept my purpose and vision ahead of me and continued the work, but in the U.S. I had more down time because the work was segmented around my trips. Enduring the pain of seeing my daughter go through years of chemotherapy was difficult, and I needed a jolt to help me in my purpose. It was at that time I decided to pursue a Ph.D. in Leadership Studies. I did not know how hard it would be to discipline myself as I traveled globally for a third of the year, was a husband and father of five, and managed an international non-profit that had projects in four countries.

From the time I started the Ph.D. program to the time I successfully defended my dissertation, the discipline to make these transformational changes was a challenge. In a sense it was like the complexities a global leader faces on a regular basis. Each day was as ambiguous as the next, and my daily priorities had to be clear.

The principle of discipline is an aspect of self-control. A leader has to discipline himself in many areas, but the two most important are time and priorities. I believe these are the most important two discipline tactics to improve the effectiveness of leaders. The leader who is disciplined accomplishes goals and objectives. Without this discipline, you might attract followers, but your long-term goals will not be met. Your development of others will be limited, and the hard work will waste away.

Principle #4 Discipline

Discipline is an aspect of self-control. A leader has to be disciplined in many areas, but the two most important are time and priorities. The leader who is disciplined with time and priorities accomplishes goals and objectives.

Virtual teams and time zone differences are some of the challenges that demand the global leader to manage time and priorities, but also the ability to lead change takes a discipline that is unique.

How does discipline manage complexities for global leaders?

In today's global economy, change happens at a frightening pace. A global leader has to discipline himself or herself to manage the speed of change. Part of leadership is not only understanding oneself but also having the ability to assess the followers' ability to perform. One of the key areas of performance in today's organization is change. For this reason, the ability to create and lead successful change projects is crucial for a leader.

Type of Complexity in Organizational Change Initiatives

Organizational leaders have to lead employees to reach the vision and mission of the organization. Leadership is the answer to change events. The first step in the change process is for the leader to make sense of the environment in order to lead through organizational change.

The complexity of the change varies, but a key aspect of successfully enduring change is centered on the effectiveness of the leader. In studying change, a challenge is to determine the type of change. Next, a leader has to determine leadership practices that match the changes needed. A common thread in change is that leading change is difficult. Leaders are faced with many challenges as organizations live in flux and chaos. During change events, global leadership practices are critical due to the increased power of the team during the change event.

When organizations experience critical change initiatives, most of the power moves to the top of the organization. Utilization of global leadership skills has a higher potential for directing the organization's short-term and long-term performance. Through strengths of vision, purpose, and effective communication, the global leader performs leadership practices that enhance the follower's ability to perform at a higher level.

Complexity #1 Organizational Change- Evolutionary

Organizational change is a planned event influenced by the environment and leadership. Although organizational theorists agree change happens, there is much debate on how change occurs in organizations. Organizational change theorists distinguish change as either episodic/continuous or revolutionary/emergent. Although there is a difference of the nature and process of change, a common theme about organizational change is that "regardless of its origin, leadership is required" (Burke, 2011, p.27).

The challenge is determining the type of leadership that is the most effective during organizational change. Burke (2011) argued that "greater integration of the standard forms of management with those from the behavioral sciences should strengthen our understanding and effectiveness of organization change methodologies and processes" (p.54). To accomplish the integration, Burke suggested that researchers need to focus on various parts of organizational change and determine how each part affects and are affected during the change process.

There are differing viewpoints on the nature of change. One view is that change is emergent, slow, and continuous, and for an organization to effectively change, a leader must focus on the small issues of change. Another view suggests that change can be small and continuous, but also episodic (one-time) and revolutionary (fast and large).

Understanding the nature of change is critical for leaders. "The problem is that management doesn't collect the proper information to develop a complete picture of what is about to happen" (Conner, 2006, p.84). To properly develop the complete picture, leaders have to understand the size of the change process. The process is based on equilibrium of our environment. When the environment is more complex than anticipated, our expectations are disrupted and the change initiative has begun.

Effective change leadership is understanding the type of resistance followers demonstrate during the change event. Organizational leaders need to understand the nature of change to assess the appropriate assimilation points. When they underestimate the amount of change the organization can endure, resistance to changes appears.

When leaders have problems assessing resistance, it is because they failed to evaluate. Evaluating the change process is not a common occurrence for organizations. "Many practitioners and change agents fail to evaluate because of the many challenges and barriers to conducting an effective and thorough evaluation" (Anderson, 2012, p. 315).

Complexity #2: Revolutionary Change

The research surrounding revolutionary change is primarily limited to political leadership, but a few research studies displayed the need to continue to research the topic. Weisberg (2010) researched the effect of revolutionary change in human resource management. Weisberg proposed that "for human resource management departments, it is more difficult to absorb and implement revolutionary influences than evolutionary ones" (p.178). The complexities that Weisberg researched are the external and internal environments that affect the organization.

Theorist such as Burke (2011) suggested that internal and external environments change at a rate that forces leaders to make changes, but the challenge is what affects an organization to make revolutionary changes? Revolutionary change occurs from a jolt to the organization that forces revolutionary change. This jolt is a change situation that "does not evolve but are more like to change in strategic orientations that demand significantly different patterns of operations" (Burke, 2011, p.75).

To better describe revolutionary change, Burke turned to the work of Gersick (1991). Multilevel research on revolutionary change shows three common domains for revolutionary change theory. The domains are deep structure, equilibrium periods, and revolutionary periods.

The first domain, deep structure, is the most critical to understanding revolutionary change but also the most difficult to define and explain. "Systems with deep structure share two characteristics: (1) they have differentiated parts and (2) the units that comprise them "work": they exchange resources with the environment in ways that maintain—and are controlled by—this differentiation" (Gersick, 1991, p.13). Burke expanded deep structure domain to describe the structure of the organization and how it makes decisions, monitors progress, and distributes power. Deep structure domains respond to the concerns of the external environment.

Equilibrium is the second domain. "If deep structure may be thought of as the design of the playing field and the rules of the game, then equilibrium periods might be compared loosely to a game in play" (Gersick, 1991, p.16). The equilibrium period is about inertia. The leaders at this point of the revolutionary change process start to experience resistance. Burke showed there are three main resistant barriers to change. They are cognition, motivation, and obligation.

The third domain is labeled the revolutionary period. "The difference between the incremental changes of equilibrium periods and revolutionary changes is like the difference between changing the game of basketball by moving the hoops higher and changing it by taking the hoops away. The first kind of change leaves the game's deep structure intact. The second dismantles it" (Gersick, 1991, p.19). During this period is when the organization feels the jolt of revolutionary change. The jolt is felt because the organizational leaders have to make decisions that decide the fate of the organization.

Whether categorizing organizational change as evolutionary or revolutionary, a global leader has to develop a disciplined lifestyle to be effective. Although I usually do a workshop on managing time and priorities, the issue of discipline goes much deeper. The type of discipline for this principle is found in endurance and perseverance. The global leader is taxed with understanding that the change process has to start, but he or she also has to assess how to identify the type of change, nature of change, and process of change. Then the leader can start developing a strategy around the assessment. The following case study is an example of the discipline needed to lead in a fast changing world.

LESSONS FROM A GLOBAL LEADER

Change in organizations is usually a frightening thought for many employees especially for those working in Asia. The company in this case study serves the poor by providing relief through educational services and distributing goods. Each day they accomplish their mission proves their resilience. With some areas of the country rapidly developing and others still stuck in extreme poverty, Asia Relief Organization (ARO) is facing a frightening future of change.

ARO is currently influencing over 50,000 people per year through their services. With this success, one would think the organization needs to stay status quo. But their vision is to expand their services to all regions, and currently they are working in only 30% of those regions. One of the major barriers to accomplishing their vision is the world is changing faster than they expected and is causing disequilibrium in the organization.

The external environment has caused donations to be minimal after the global crisis of 2008. Most of the employees come from the capital city, which is seeing growth, but it is causing an increase in the standard of living. The increase in cost means ARO has to pay higher salaries to retain employees. The challenge is how to restructure the organization to reach all of the regions in Asia. In the midst of the restructuring, there is another challenge of transitioning to local leadership.

Background

The fast changes in the external environment and the increased pressure for their services caused a fright throughout the organization. Culturally there is anxiety when there is fast change, which causes what Conner (2006) terms as the beast. "The beast is the fear and anxiety within us all as we encounter the significant, unanticipated changes that shatter our expectations. It is not a figment of the imagination, and it cannot be explained away as a passing phase that afflicts only a young boy or a frightened soldier. The Beast is a metaphor, but its devastation of individuals, organizations, and society is real" (Conner, 2006, p.27).

For the staff at ARO, an actual beast continues to haunt the leadership in the organization. There is a good reason why they are not as accepting of quick change like the west is used to. Since ARO is a U.S. based organization, they had to understand the nature of the beast in Asia to accomplish the task of change and meet the current demands on the organization. To ARO's credit, they focused on the resilience of the remarkable people in Asia.

Challenges to ARO's Vision

The resiliency of the ARO's staff to face frightening disorder in the organization started a few years ago. The staggering event that forced strategic changes in the organization was losing a major donor at the beginning of the global crisis. This caused the organization to go from over 200 to 120 employees. The loss of funding caused a shuffling of top leadership. The four expatriate leaders who were managing the Asian staff were reduced to one expatriate leader.

The senior management team made up of only Asians took over as the country director for ARO. They were tasked with increasing the 62,000 people currently impacted to 100,000 people while reducing staff due to losing 20% of their budget. Serving more people and regaining the momentum to accomplish their vision requires expanding into new regions. Over the last four years, they have only entered one new province.

Needed changes in ARO

One of the primary steps for leaders in an organization is learning to diagnose the need for change. ARO needed to assess how they were attaining their desired goals, the efficiency of their services, and the ability of their human resources to cope with change.

ARO was stagnant, not moving forward in reaching their desired goals. Another ineffectiveness of their system was their inability to cope with changes in the environment. ARO started operations in the early 1990s. At the time many countries in Asia were extremely poor and underdeveloped. Now, many parts of the region are developing quickly. The needs of the people are changing along with the expectations of employees. Working for a nongovernment organization like ARO had been a prized job in many developing countries in Asia, but now they do not even pay the average salary for educated employees.

As shown through the short assessment, it is obvious there needed to be changes throughout the ARO organization. The challenge was how could ARO implement the change process by utilizing the resilience of the staff instead of experiencing hostilities and resistance?

Resilience in Orchestrating Change

As the change initiative proceeded forward, ARO had to discover the structure of change. ARO needed to focus on three primary areas of resilience in order to have effective change in the organization. They were the nature, process, and roles of change. These three areas would develop the pattern needed to implement effective change.

Nature of Change

Understanding the nature of change is critical for ARO. Global leaders need to see the complete picture of what is happening to cause the disequilibrium. To properly develop the complete picture, ARO has to understand the size of the change process. This means the leadership has to decide if the nature of change is minor or major. With more disruption to the day-to-day life of the staff, the change process increases in intensity. ARO's effectiveness in change depends on the resilience of the staff. To determine the resilience, ARO must assimilate the change initiative, which is understanding the process of positive and negative implications of the change event. Since the staff has encountered so much change in the past few years, it is important for ARO to properly assess the assimilation points.

Why will there be resistance to change from ARO?

Over the last few years, the ARO organization has made leadership decisions that have caused disruptions along with natural and economic circumstances. Each type of decision has caused resistance in various ways. One of the more prominent reactions has been staff and volunteers going to new organizations.

To understand the resistance more clearly, it is important to detail the eight phases of emotional response to disruption that Conner (2006) describes along with his change process. Emotions play a large part in the resistance to change. The challenge for ARO is to identify the phases so they can better serve their staff, volunteers, partners, and community.

Phase I- Stability represents the status quo.

Phase II- Immobilization is when the "initial reaction to a negatively perceived change is shock" (Conner, 2006, p.133). Three main situations have caused shock in the organization. The first change was losing the major donor and having to disband a major project in the organization. The second was the change in expatriate staff. The third change was the formation of the senior management team made up of four Asians.

Phase III- Denial is "characterized by an inability to assimilate new information into the current frame of reference" (p.133).

Phase IV- Anger is demonstrated by "frustration and hurt, often manifested through irrational, indiscriminate lashing out" (p.134). During these changes, many leaders on staff have struggled with anger. Lashing out is an all too common phenomenon and has caused much hurt in the organization.

Phase V- Bargaining is when "people begin negotiating to avoid the negative impact of change" (p.134). For ARO, bargaining has occurred in forming relationships of power. The leader-member exchange has increased.

Phase VI- Depression is a normal response to negatively perceived change. "Resignation to failure, feeling victimized, a lack of emotional and physical energy, and disengagement" (p.135) are forms of organizational depression. This type of organizational depression is rampant throughout ARO. This is the primary reason they have not experienced growth over the last two years.

Phase VII- Testing phase is when people start feeling back in control of their situation. To the observer of the organization, one would say ARO has not entered Phase VII. The senior management team still needs outside influence to make decisions, and they still complain about their lack of power to make decisions.

Phase VIII- Acceptance is when "targets now respond to the change realistically" (p.135). Among the staff, there is a growing acceptance of Asians leading the organization instead of Americans. The problem is through Phases IV, V, and VI there is so much hurt that the current senior management team cannot gain acceptance.

Process of Change

In determining the assimilation points for change in ARO, the leadership team is taxed with planning the process in which the change will take place. In the transition of change, resilient people understand there is chaos around change, and they are disciplined to work through the chaos. For many Asians this is an everyday experience with just driving to work. Traffic patterns in parts of Asia change by the minute. It is a fluid exercise just to arrive at work. A 5-kilometer trip can take 20 minutes. This is why their day-to-day assimilation is lower at times because each day is different.

Due to the day-to-day grind of living in the developing world, a new measure of pain has to be enacted by leadership in order to start the transition. To understand the challenge that ARO faced, it is important to identify the pain and remedy of the change process.

What is the Pain Message?

Pain in the change process is a jolt or an event that justifies breaking the status quo and moving forward. For ARO, the pain is the information of bad employee performances that led to loss of funds, projects, volunteers, and staff. With the loss of these critical areas, they are not able to serve the current communities, nor are they able to grow into new communities.

How does pain drive change? For ARO, the pain of not reaching communities with their services should drive the staff to desire change. This type of change would encourage sacrifice like following an outsider, even an international leader or a local who has a business background. Hiring from within has not worked for the past three years, so the choices are limited.

What is the Remedy?

The remedy for ARO is an action plan that solves a problem or makes the most of the opportunity the change initiative has created. Their remedy has to take the organization from the transition state of having a part-time facilitator in charge to the desired state of having a full-time country director. The opportunity in this remedy is to overhaul the organizational structure in order to create a better way to develop organizational leaders. The action of changing from an insider in the organization to an outsider is just one step of the larger process.

To take advantage of this opportunity, there has to be designated roles. The leadership of the change process has to define roles and responsibilities. In the end, the change that starts out as minor, ends with a major shift in the organizational structure to develop more effective leaders that will propel the organization toward the goal of working in all provinces.

Roles of Change

Global leaders who exhibit resilience during change initiatives make critical decisions understanding that everyone involved in the organization are impacted by the decisions. For this reason, it is imperative for ARO to properly identify the roles. The best option in defining roles during the change initiative is not to follow a linear path but instead gather people throughout the organization and empower them with a voice in the discussion. Because of cultural reasons, ARO followed a linear path.

What are the roles?

The primary role in the change process is the sponsor. A few of the primary characteristics for this role are:

I.   Power is critical in the change process because people respect power differently in the Asian culture.
II. Pain is part of the reason the sponsors make the decision to change. The sponsor feels the pain like the followers. The desire to reach the vision of the organization drives the pain to reality.
III. Vision accomplishes the piece of the change process that shows the followers where the organization is going. For ARO, survival is not enough. Their vision is to continue growing the organization.
IV. Monitoring plans is not micro-managing, but instead they are engaged in the process. The sponsors make sure they stay apprised of the developments of the organization. This is a main area ARO has struggled in as an organization.
V.   A willingness to sacrifice for the vision is what followers want to see in their sponsors. This is an important aspect for current ARO leaders. Will the sponsors sacrifice for the vision? Will they make the decisions that take endurance to enact?

Resilience in Enduring Change

After developing the change process and implementing the change process, the final step is enduring the difficulties to see the change effect take place. The importance of resilience increases during this stage. Sponsors, targets, and agents have to meet the challenges, such as resistance, pain and remedy, and setbacks in the change process since "strategic resilience is not about responding to a onetime crisis. It's not about rebounding from a setback. It's about continuously anticipating and adjusting to deep, secular trends" (Burke, 2009, p.513).

The problem is the world is growing more volatile quicker than ARO is becoming more resilient. The pace of change ARO has undertaken over the last five years is a great example of how fast the world is changing in developing countries. To increase resilience in enduring change, there are four challenges all organizations must address.

1. The cognitive challenge - "The company must become entirely free of denial, nostalgia, and arrogance. It must be deeply conscious of what's changing and perpetually willing to consider how those changes are likely to affect is current success" (Burke, p.514)
2. The strategic challenge - "The ability to create a plethora of new options as compelling alternatives to dying strategies" (p.514).
3. The political challenge - "An organization must be able to divert resources from yesterday's products and programs to tomorrow's" (p.515).
4. The ideological challenge - "If renewal is to become continuous and opportunity-driven, rather than episodic and crisis-driven, companies will need to embrace a creed that extends beyond operational excellence and flawless execution" (Burke, 515).

ARO faces all four barriers to strategic resilience during their current change process. It is important to review each barrier in context with the progress of ARO's change initiative.

1. ARO is a humble organization, but they live in a dangerous nostalgia. The last 20 years has brought great success to their projects in Asia, but the region has changed, which is causing the problems in their organizational structure. ARO has to forget the past and look more strategically into the future.
2. Some of the core strategies at ARO are dying. They have to develop new strategies that can propel them into all provinces. "Resilience depends on variety" (p.519).

3. Nostalgia also creates the barrier for the political challenge. The legacy programs have been an effective promotional material for ARO, but they are not allowing the organization to grow because the legacy programs are resource heavy. "To be resilient, businesses must minimize their propensity to overfund legacy strategies" (p.523).

4. ARO ideology creates their episodic and crisis-driven culture. Much of their organization is responding to crisis events so it is not surprising that their organization has a crisis-driven culture. Part of their organizational change has to address this problem. They have to identify how to change the crisis-driven culture into an opportunity-driven culture.

These barriers to resilience are prominent at ARO. By having the barrier and problems associated with nostalgia, it only increases the challenges to enduring the change. This increase places more of the burden on leaders during the post-launch of the change initiative.

Leading after launch of change initiative

As in all situations of change, leadership is critical. For organizations during the post-launch phase of change, leaders are again challenged in ways that separate leaders from managers. ARO has experienced this issue over the last few years after the post-launch of organizational change.

Leaders have to diversify the strategy for change. Using multiple leverages is important because change is too complex for only one plan. Leaders have to choose many actions and not just stop one action such as organizational structure change. For ARO, the change is not just about moving local leaders into the country director role, but they also need a new organizational structure to expand their vision at a faster rate.

Another factor is leaders have to take responsibility for the decisions. Not everyone will be happy with change, so the change leader will be challenged. Pushback from the change initiative is to be expected. "These are the times when the change leader must use as much self-control as she or he can muster, working hard (1) to listen, (2) not to be defensive, and (3) to display the patience of Job" (Burke, 2009, p.752). For ARO, the regional leader has not been willing to take the heat and listen. Instead, there are people who are defensive and avoid talking to each other when trying to find a solution.

The change leader also has to show consistency. As followers monitor the change leader, they are looking for authenticity and decisions not based on the latest fad that quickly changes. Passiveness in change situations causes leaders to look inconsistent. ARO's leadership team has to move away from passive aggressive behavior and be authentic and consistent with decisions.

The fourth action of a change leader during the post-launch stage of the change initiative is perseverance. The first part of organizational change is much easier than the end. Change leaders must have the discipline to stay the course and encourage others to persevere.

The final action for the change leader is to repeat the message. "The message is the vision and the mission, but to be most effective a story needs to be told that incorporates the vision and mission and values" (Burke, 2009, p.753). The change process is a message that reads like a narrative of the change effort's progress. It needs updating with fresh stories to remind followers why they are making the changes in the organization. Repeating the message is critical to learning the story.

ARO has not persevered during the changes. The message is changing along with the actions. Because of the inconsistency, they continue to find themselves in the situation where people are leaving the organization. With losing staff, they are not close to expanding to another region and therefore are not on course to reaching their goals.

7

COMPASSION

In 2000 I walked out of a meeting in Cairo, Egypt and felt something new. I have always loved to help people, but this time was different. The meeting in Cairo was for a group of Egyptian, lower-class citizens. They were looking for help to open up small entrepreneurial businesses to achieve a greater purpose of serving those in need. When I left the meeting, we did not come up with one solution or one plan to help these men. My heart sank, and I felt horrible. It was at that point when I felt the last principle of compassion the strongest. My compassion has only grown over the years as I have traveled the world and met other groups looking for opportunities to grow in leadership to serve those in need.

2010 was a transition year with us moving back to America, and my discipline was tested further by starting a Ph.D. degree. I also added a new long-term project in the country of India. One of the organizations we chose to work with was an established relief organization whose mission was to serve poor and underprivileged children in India. They had hostels to educate and develop young people to bring them out of the bondage of severe poverty.

The organization had been in existence for over 30 years and was working with communities throughout India, serving tens of thousands of children. The project we started was an eight-month leadership development program that consisted of four separate trainings, developing an action plan, live exercises, and coaching. The goal was to expose these twelve participants to organizational leadership situations in order to determine which four or five could be selected as potential candidates for the country executive director role.

As always, I grow personally while I serve these wonderful people during the project. To hear about the conditions and environments these leaders work in and how they overcome the challenges and obstacles on a regular basis to achieve their mission was refreshing and convicting. It made my daily challenges and obstacles seem miniscule.

For example, I was exhausted from my long trip from Dallas to India. It takes me around 24 hours from when I leave my house in Dallas to when I arrive at a hotel in India. But many of the participants traveled as long as 30 hours on slow moving trains to attend the workshops! As much as I complain about flying economy, the seats these guys have in crowded Indian trains make my economy seat look like first class.

Over the eight months, I was able to bond with the participants and really felt like we helped them grow as leaders. We also achieved our goal of identifying the five future executive leaders in the group. The time with this organization was rewarding and challenging.

In India it is common at the closing of the workshop for the participants to stand and share what they learned and experienced from the teaching. One of the seasoned leaders stood, and I was astonished by what he said. He spoke the usual words of gratitude and then said, "In my thirty-five years of working for this organization, this is the first time I've been taught about leadership, and I am so thankful for the training."

This is why I sacrifice and discipline - to hear these words and know I am fulfilling my purpose. My compassion for this group was the glue that kept the process going. I know that using the word compassion is not common when discussing leadership, but I will explain how compassion will help global leaders manage the complexities they face in their leadership.

The Principle: Compassion

The final leadership principle is compassion. Compassion is centered on an emotional intelligence (EI). Compassion is extremely important in becoming a leader and in developing new leaders for the next generation.

Of all the soft skills I have written about, this is the most extreme soft skill. A leader struggles without compassion because the essence of leadership is being able to develop more leaders. Without the leadership principle of compassion, a leader will struggle to effectively and successfully develop others.

This is the leadership principle I admire most in a global leader. As a follower, compassion is a principle I look for in a leader. A quote by Martin Luther King, Jr. (2003) describes the leadership principle of compassion:

"Everybody can be great... because anybody can serve. You don't have to have a college degree to serve. You don't have to make your subject and verb agree to serve. You only need a heart full of grace. A soul generated by love."

The heart of a compassionate global leader is servanthood. A true leader asks, "How can I serve you?" The ability to ask this question comes from the principle of compassion. Leaders must have and show qualities that others admire.

Principle #5 Compassion

Compassion is extremely important in becoming a leader and in developing new leaders for the next generation. Of all the soft skills I have written about, this is the most extreme soft skill, but a leader struggles without it because the essence of leadership is being able to develop more leaders. Without the leadership principle of compassion, a leader will struggle to develop others.

Compassion is a hard trait to exhibit in a leaders' own culture and even more so in multiple cultures. How a global leader communicates to and treats the next generation of leaders is as important as the process. A wrong word or cultural insensitivity can cause a leader to be labeled as weak or hegemonistic. Both are damaging to relationships and decrease the effectiveness of leadership.

How does Compassion help manage complexities for global leader?

The two attributes of a global leader that must be paired with compassion to be able to manage complexities are sensemaking and emotional intelligence

(EI). The global leader has to make sense of the situation in order to begin to exhibit compassion. This is a cognitive skill and not only a soft skill. The global leader has to learn to make decisions understanding the impact it will have on many people's lives.

Another critical attribute of a compassionate leader is emotional intelligence. EI can be understood in many contexts, but for a global leader the most important circumstance to understand one's emotional intelligence in when working in teams. For global leaders working in virtual and cross-cultural teams, exhibiting emotional intelligence is critical to develop the leaders on the team.

Sensemaking

Sensemaking is a similar process to global leadership because the descriptions of both use words such as ambiguity, technology, feelings/emotions, and disorientation to change. All global leaders will go through this type of psychological roller coaster, and to manage the complexity one needs to make sense of the situation with compassion embedded in the thought process.

Sensemaking comes before decision-making. In the complexity of global leadership, there is chaos. A leader uses sensemaking to organize in the chaos. Leaders find effects of sensemaking whenever the current situation is perceived as different from their expected situation.

Leaders talk organizations into existence. One of the main acts as a leader is to clearly communicate the vision and goals of the group and to transform the group. The principle of compassion ensures there is a thought process before the action.

Sensemaking is important to the principle of compassion. The connection between sensemaking and compassion is in the 'social context'. The global leader has to organize information and make sequences in their decisions. The global leader has to perform the act of sensemaking with compassion. Three core elements of sensemaking for global leaders are the ability to explore a wider system, create a map of the current system, and change the system to learn more about the organization.

Many integral parts synthesize sensemaking into global leadership. The main part is in the context of crisis and how a leader makes sense of crisis events. In the context of crisis, the essential elements in sensemaking are commitment, identity, and expectations. Identity is especially important for global leaders who exhibit the principle of compassion. The process in which a follower identifies the leader will dictate their willingness to follow.

The complexity for global leaders is when a follower's identity dictates the follower's decisions. For example, an Indian from a lower social status will not be as aggressive in decision making if an Indian from a higher social status is on the team. The global leader has to exhibit compassion to serve the follower. The compassion starts with first making sense of the situation before making quick judgments or statements that the leader will regret. When a global leader receives an email full of criticism, the decision is whether to respond quickly with harsh words or think through the implications of this type of communication. An effective global leader will pause and make sense of the entire situation before replying.

EI in Leadership

Along with sensemaking the compassionate leader needs to exhibit a high emotional intelligence. Becoming a compassionate leader depends on a global leader's emotional intelligence. To decipher emotional intelligence, one must first start with the domains of the competencies associated with EI. The competencies are segmented into two areas, personal and social. Under personal competence, the domains are self-awareness, which is knowing your strengths and weaknesses, and self-management, which is a desire to achieve and meet personal goals. For social competence, the domains are social awareness, which is meeting needs of followers, and relationship management, which is listening to others to encourage them toward a better performance.

Not only do global leaders have to understand their own emotions, but they must be able to effectively communicate these emotions in a clear purpose. Intuition helps the leader make strategic decisions to enhance the effectiveness of the purpose. Although using statistics is important in strategic planning, a global leader has to use intuition while making plans and decisions.

For a global leader, the intuition gained from self-awareness and self-management is crucial, but when these skills are combined in a global team, there are more challenges, especially when the people on the team are leaders in the organization. To ascertain the specific challenges for a global leader working in teams, one needs to combine self-awareness and self-management with the primary responsibilities of top management teams.

EI and Global Teams

Global teams are now the rule instead of the exception. A global team is defined by diversity throughout the teamwork process, which means diverse cultures, nations, and geographic locations. Research on global teams found that a deep structural network of diverse backgrounds increases the probability of better performance for the global leader.

Cohesiveness generates alignment in a global team, which increases the performance of the team members. Failure to build cohesiveness in a team results in members not aligned to the organization's goals and purpose. Alignment provided by cohesiveness builds resonance that attracts followers to the vision. Cohesiveness generated in global teams comes from a compassionate leader.

To develop compassion as a global leader, there has to be an understanding of emotional intelligence. From the list of emotional intelligence characteristics, there are two that global teams benefit from the most. "From self-awareness - understanding one's emotions and being clear about one's purpose - flows self-management, the focused drive that all leaders need to achieve their goals" (Goleman, Boyatzis, & McKee, 2002, p. 45). When leaders have control over emotions and self-management, they are more adaptable to changing environments and overcoming obstacles. Another important trait of a self-managed leader is transparency, which provides trustworthiness, honesty, and integrity.

When researching whether emotional intelligence creates alignment and resonance in global teams, it is critical to describe common leadership practices of the global team. The characteristics that relate to the emotionally intelligent leader are strategic decisions, social networks, and culture of innovation. Global teams have an important role to play in these areas, which improves the performance of organizations.

Self-Awareness

Global teams make decisions that affect the short and long-term performance of the organization. In making these strategic decisions, leaders need to listen to the perspective of everyone on the team. Leaders in global teams have to identify synergies. The identification process of the synergies is contingent on breaking down psychological and social psychological barriers in order to gain buy-in to the decisions made by the team.

Social networking is another area that dictates performance of global teams. A social network refers to both internal and external networks in the organization. To optimize social networks, a compassionate leader manages complexity in global leadership by developing a strong cohesion in their social networks.

Self-Management

Another important characteristic of global teams is the influence on leadership dynamics specifically in organizational innovation. The global leader should have an advantage in organizational innovation because he or she can channel viewpoints from so many backgrounds and develop an engine of innovation. The ability to channel the viewpoints of a diverse global team comes from the discipline of self-management.

A global leader uses his self-management skills to promote a clear vision for the organization, which improves team effectiveness. Through effective communication within the team, the global leader creates emotions that increase energy and motivation in order for the team to reach a higher level of performance.

It is difficult to properly define soft terms like compassion, but I have used sensemaking and emotional intelligence to describe concrete ways compassion is effective in global leadership. These actions will help a global leader manage the complexities faced specifically in global teams as shown by the following lesson from a global leader.

LESSONS FROM A GLOBAL LEADER

One of the main goal of leadership is to inspire others to become a valuable asset to society and to reach beyond their expectations of themselves. The question is how do we inspire? Inspiration comes from having compassion for your followers, a type of compassion that comes from emotional and spiritual intelligence.

Compassionate Leadership

According to the United Nations' *World Population Prospects* (2011), the world population will reach 7 billion people on October 31st, 2011. The increase in population since the turn of the 21st century is almost 1 billion people. With the enormous population growth, the complexities of serving communities in need have also increased. The Food and Agriculture Organization of the United Nations (2010) reported that 925 million people currently live in undernourished conditions. Such a large burden has made it difficult for social activist to meet the needs of the communities. The challenge for these global leaders is to attract and develop future leaders who can create vision, share values, and grow the organization in order to make an impact in the fast growing world. At a time when the world is seeing natural disasters, poverty, human trafficking, and many other social challenges, the pressure on social activist to perform at a high level is coming from donors, boards, partners, and, most of all, the needy in the communities.

Therefore, social activist and entrepreneurs have to develop new strategies in order to obtain, develop, and empower future leaders to tackle the many challenges facing these organizations. Although a few social entrepreneurs and their organizations, such as Teach for America, have been able to obtain talent from top schools, the standard social entrepreneur does not have the ability to recruit leaders categorized as intelligent, according to scholastic tests and other measures of IQ testing, from business schools and other educational institutions. For social entrepreneurs to succeed, they must first understand what aspects of intelligence are drivers to developing the type of leaders that perform at the highest levels.

Peter Drucker urges social entrepreneurs to "keep your eye on the task, not on yourself. The task matters, and you are a servant" (Drucker, 1990, p.27). To comply with such wisdom, leaders need a certain type of intelligence to serve their organization, but what type of intelligence? This is especially important for social activist where leadership is about a task and not rewarded by prestige or income like in sectors that recruit the classical intelligent person.

Crutchfield and McLeod Grant (2008) researched social entrepreneurs and their impact on their communities and discovered that leadership is extremely important to social entrepreneurship. They view leadership more critical because they are service organizations that invest most of their money on one asset - their employees. This means the programs and services for social organizations are bound by the talent they hire and retain.

Other research in the social entrepreneurship industry has also yielded a connection between leadership and performance. The effective leader in a social entrepreneurship organization translates caring, believing, and compassion into results. From these results the social entrepreneurship organizations are able to expand their capacity to reach more people with their vision and mission. A study in the workbook from the Center of Creative Leadership says that a way to produce growth is to expand the capacity of leaders in the organization who not only can develop their own abilities but also develop the leadership ability of their teams and communities.

To coincide with the increased awareness of different intelligences, social entrepreneurship and the organizations they start have seen dramatic growth. The National Center for Charitable Statistics (2011) reported that U.S. nonprofit organizations reported over $1.44 trillion in total revenues and $1.34 trillion in total expenses from over 1.6 million charitable organizations. With this growth in numbers and more competition for funding, the need has increased for social entrepreneurs and their organizations to recruit, retain, and develop leaders. "And studies show that the social sector is facing an impending leadership crisis. Just as demand is growing, supply is falling due to the number of baby boomers retiring, a high rate of burnout among social entrepreneur executives, and the failure of most organizations to develop human resources within their organization" (Crutchfield & McLeod Grant, 2008, pp.176-177).

Leaders who are looking to make a difference in the world have many challenges. These challenges are not easy to solve, and it takes more than a traditional view of intelligence. Global leaders seeking to make a difference in the world need to be driven by a compassion for followers and the people they serve. Their intelligence is not being able to get the most from people but instead being able to give the most to people.

Another type of Intelligence

As I described earlier in this chapter, compassion is generated through an emotional intelligence, and that compassionate intuition helps develop strategic plans and implementation for the organization and especially for global teams. From researching intelligences, there is a deeper intelligence that creates our intuition. It is a spiritual intelligence.

Clint Sidle expanded the idea of intelligence and leadership as the director of the Roy H. Park Leadership Fellows Program in the Johnson School of Management at Cornell University. His ideas and research on leadership and intelligence add another characteristic of intelligence. Sidle's (2007) research was based on the fact of so many ethical failures in leadership, which led to his view that it is time to change the paradigm of leadership and seek to develop leaders who will do good for society.

The framework of his theory was not based on empirical data similar to Sternberg, but it came from the document review of a study performed by anthropologists as they studied indigenous cultures across the world. The study found that cultures share similar beliefs about the effectiveness of man. Their beliefs were put into the shape of cardinal directions of the compass with four or five archetypal intelligences. Other names for this compass are Mandala or Medicine Wheel. This framework has guided these cultures for thousands of years concerning personal growth and effectiveness.

All five of the intelligences are similar to many modern concepts of leadership; "the key difference, however, is the utter simplicity and intuitive appeal the five intelligences have for understanding leadership and how to develop leaders who do well while doing good for the world" (Sidle, 2007, p.20).

The main difference in Sidle's research is the inclusion of another intelligence called spiritual intelligence (SIQ). SIQ poses great interest in the study of social activist since their work is based on a cause or a belief system. Sidle describes spiritual leaders as those who are effective because they are zealous in the development of their skills as leaders (Sidle, 2007).

Leadership and Spiritual Intelligence

A common misunderstanding is that most people think about social activism and leadership only within charitable organizations. This assumption is wrong. For-profit organization needs spiritual intelligence also. The following scenario is from a conglomerate of situations I have witnessed in serving organizations around the world. The point of this exercise is for you to view how spiritual intelligence can help leaders grow in their compassionate leadership. From this growth, followers in all organizations will benefit, and the world will have leaders that are more impactful for the good of society.

A Spiritually Intelligent Business Model

Sensemaking is when a person has to assess a situation because the actual is different from the expected. For Tim, the actual was that he thought fresh drinking water was available to everyone. In Tim's first trip to Asia, he came to understand that millions of people do not have access to fresh water. According to Unicef (2014), over 1,000 children die every day with a waterborne illness. Unicef also estimates that over 700 million people do not have access to clean drinking water. This is more than twice the population of the U.S.

So Tim started communicating his thoughts, and an organization was born with a vision to bring fresh drinking water to people around the world. The vision was full of compassion, but it would take global leadership skills to implement the vision. The first step was planning how to raise the funds for the company. One option was becoming a charitable organization, but Tim did not have a non-profit background, so he chose a for-profit business model.

Because he chose a for-profit business model, Tim needed to raise funds to start the business. In creating the business plan, Tim did not lose his compassion by projecting financials that would burden the organization with his profit expectations that would increase prices of the product. He knew if the price increased, it would reduce the availability of the product.

Once he was able to secure a limited amount of funds, he had to develop a product on a low budget. This took EI, self-management and self-awareness. He could not do this alone, but he did not have funds to pay other engineers. So Tim started sharing his vision with fellow engineers. From his compassionate words in describing the current situation of clean water availability, engineers started to donate their time to help Tim. In 6 months, they developed a prototype that worked.

The challenge was how to distribute the product to villages around the world. Most of the target market was in difficult places in Asia and Africa. A traditional distribution model would increase the cost of the product and reduce the amount of villages that could afford the product. But Tim had to also think about his organization and make profits. So the practical and compassionate worlds collide. Tim needed to learn how to become a global leader. His spiritual intelligence increased his compassion to learn new methods of distribution.

In Tim's travels around Africa, he came up with the solution. He went back to his engineers and asked to develop a product that could be assembled by parts that are accessible in Africa. He then invested in small manufacturers in each country that would make the product. This not only lowered the cost of the product but also created jobs.

Conclusion

This story of Tim demonstrates the power of compassionate leadership. Although I used a fictional character, I have met many people like Tim around the world. The problem is more leaders are not like Tim. Their plans are filled with self-gain instead of compassion. The development of the leadership principle compassion can be inspirational and challenging to a global leader. Having the ability to make sense of the environment and use compassion as an emotional intelligence takes a self-aware leader who knows that they have to conquer personal issues that prevent compassion.

PART 3

Development of Global Leaders

8

DEVELOPING THE FIVE
LEADERSHIP PRINCIPLES

Now that I have described the five principles to help global leaders manage complexities, the final piece of the puzzle is the development of these principles. What I have learned in my 15 years of training and development work around the world is that no two stones are alike. Meaning, each organization I walk into has a unique culture and set of needs for their leadership development just like individuals each have unique finger prints.

Because of the unique needs of each organization, leadership development is not similar to training hard skills, such as computer knowledge or accounting. Leadership development requires training, experiential knowledge, and self-learning. In this chapter, I will show the importance of learning and development, the progress in global leadership development, and a few practical ways to develop the five principles of global leadership.

Learning and Development

I was recently at a conference where Barbara Kellerman spoke. She made an astute observation. We are in an unprecedented age of leadership studies, yet we have the most ineffective and toxic leaders. Why is this happening?

The more I thought about this observation, the more I agreed. Leadership gurus, books, and educational opportunities are accessible around the world, but why are we having so many leadership problems. In the field of academic and practical leadership studies, we do a great job of detailing effective leadership, but we are still only at the surface in understanding how to develop effective global leaders. In order to prove my point, we need to take a deeper survey of leadership development. If you believe, like me, that leaders can be developed, it is important to understand the constructionist view of leadership development. One of the main catalysts to constructionist thought in learning is Vygotsky and his theory of Zone of Proximal Development.

Constructionist View of Leadership Development

A constructionist explains leadership as "one or more individuals in a social system who succeed in framing and defining how the demands of the group will be taken up and who will address the need for direction in the collective action" (Goethals, 2007, p. 190). Constructivism views leaders as strengthening their abilities over time through a developmental process. Three areas stand out that connect the constructionist view of leadership development. They are social, cultural, and 'meaning-making' processes (Goethals, 2007, p. 191). The process of development in leadership for a constructionist is performed in community.

By utilizing Vygotsky's theory of learning and development, one can make the connection to leadership development. Vygotsky used a triangle to symbolize the development process. The triangle consisted of the subject and goal on the base while the mediating tool was at the point. The action triangle represents a single person who is labeled the subject. The subject is performing an action that has a goal. Some types of mediating tools influence the subject's ability to reach the goal. For leaders the mediating tools show how they think, feel, and behave (Gold, 2010). Leadership gives a perfect example of the most important mediating tool, which is language. Language requires the leader to interact in the society. So the leader utilizes the tool of language to reach the goal. For example, a leader wants to change a certain process in the team, so he calls a meeting. In the meeting the leader needs to communicate to the team that they will have a new process. The leader's goal is to change the behavior of the team. The leader must then use the mediating tool of language to reach the goal (Gold, 2010, p. 275).

Leadership is a unique type of meaning making process compared with more general cognitive processes that are part of human life. This is so because the sharing agreements that produce leadership are articulated and generated within a community practice,, a group working to achieve results. Since leadership requires a social setting and mediating tools to communicate, an extreme amount of importance is placed on culture and primary language. In today's global environment, the importance of communicating across cultures, time zones, and countries causes many problems and decreases effectiveness for organizations. For this reason organizations are increasing learning opportunities for their employees that create a better working environment in a constructive worldview.

With this challenge for leaders in the global economy, Vygotsky's work on thought and language can help. His work on creativity and active thought uses the phrase *egocentric speech* or *inner speech*. The challenge for leaders in a multicultural setting is that they are confident with their inner speech but lack confidence in using a mediating tool such as a second language. With inner speech the leader is able to think and discuss a plan with himself and then communicate the plan. All of these functions are highly important, and if leaders were developed to increase their self-regulation of inner speech in a format that would allow for better communication to the team of the plan, the leader would see more success in meeting goals.

The final piece is the developmental process where constructionism views leadership development not as "a fixed phenomenon, or a set of qualities that belong to an individual, but as meaning making; leadership is an emergent phenomenon that develops in community, over time" (Goethals, 2007, p. 194). By identifying leadership as happening in community and over time, the job of leader can be accomplished by anyone. This is closely akin to Vygotsky's view of development. Even children who live on the streets, have a handicap, or live in a rural setting have a chance to learn and develop according to Vygotsky. Today, a constructionist will say anyone has the ability to lead in his or her community. In order to learn to lead, it will take a dynamic social process (Goethals, 2007, p. 190). The process is learned in collaboration and is activity based.

ZPD in Leadership Development

Utilizing Vygotsky's (1986) definition of ZPD, the distance between the actual development level of independent problem-solving and the potential development determined through collaboration, organizations can develop their leaders using Vygotsky's writings. To refer back to the action triangle, leaders need a toolbox of mediating tools to reach their goals in today's complex environment. Vygotsky believed that the essence of development was the mastering of *auxiliary stimuli*, to gain operation of cognitive thought that would not be possible in a natural process. As pointed out before in Vygotsky's stages of mastery and self-regulation, there was a transformation from the premastery stage, which was absent of self-regulation, to the ultimate outcome of self-organized attention and conceptual thinking. This transformation was contingent on the child's motivation to go through each stage. Leadership development goes through this same process. A person starts at a premastery stage, and the goal is to reach the ultimate outcome - to be a confident conceptual thinker on issues concerning leadership. The transformation through the stages of leadership development follows the same requirement, and the main push through these stages is the motivation of the person being developed. As with Vygotsky's theory, a person's motivation can be easily measured once they are placed in the zone. The fact ZPD can help identify the readiness to learn promotes an accountability system to the organization that is investing money to train the potential leader.

For the ZPD to be successful in leadership development, it requires the same attention between expert and novice as with teacher and student. How would you categorize a person as an expert in leadership? Does having leadership knowledge give one the ability to develop leaders? Does only having leadership experience give one the right to develop leaders? These are the questions human resource departments face in today's leader development paradigm along with the fact that society, culture, and history play a part in the learning process, so there is real world activity. How does an outsider to the organization teach leadership issues? The answer is in the utilization of Vygotsky's theories and providing a collaborative, participant-centered environment that creates a learning environment with activity-based learning.

In order to combine the theories of Vygotsky into the leadership development programs, first you start with action learning.

> Action learning is a win/win individual and company approach to learning and development that at the same time is capable of resolving significant business, organizational, and social problems. It is a form of learning through experience, 'by doing,' where the job environment is the classroom (Smith, 2001, p. 35).

Many organizations have implemented an action-learning environment in their trainings. Vygotsky used the terms *scientific* and *spontaneous concepts* to separate what is learned in a classroom and how a person learns in a social environment.

The strength of scientific concepts lies in their conscious and deliberate character. Spontaneous concepts, on the contrary, are strong in what concerns the situational, empirical, and practical. These two conceptual systems, developing 'from above' and 'from below', reveal their real nature in the interrelations between actual development and the zone of proximal development.

Vygotsky's conceptual systems align with a leadership development model that utilizes training by a teacher and action learning by the group. The key in the effectiveness of the spontaneous concepts would be to mix the social and cultural background in the learning in order to provide active learning experiences where the learner uses historical concepts. The onus is on the teacher to just provide the learning environment for the leader, which alleviates the pressure for the teacher to be an expert in all fields.

Although the person is individually responsible for learning the skills and abilities of a leader, the more the development can focus on group projects the more successful the development of the leader. Again, there is a connection with the constructionist learning techniques of student centered and group focused. The leadership development program using ZPD would focus on the student while using activities that provide a group setting to solve real life problems for the participants. This collaboration allows for the discussion of more experiences and for the use of more mediating tools by the leader.

Global Leadership Development

In the early 1990s, organizations started to expand globally, but their human resource capacity did not keep up with business strategy (Holt & Seki, 2012). In response, consultants and researchers started to explore the development of global leaders. In 1998, Gregersen et al. was one of the first to attempt to define a global leadership development construct. Gergersen et al. (1998) conducted research from 1994-1997 by interviewing 130 executives in 50 organizations.

Gregersen et al. (1998) found four strategies for developing global leaders. The first strategy is for the global leader to travel and learn firsthand about the customer or people. The second is to establish diverse teams that work successfully together. The third strategy is training in which the global leader learns in a structured environment. The fourth and most effective development strategy is to transfer the global leader to work on an international assignment.

Suutari (2002) reviewed literature on global leadership development and identified the topic as an emerging research agenda. The most common developmental process at the time was international assignments, short-term development assignments, international teams, action learning groups, training, and meetings and forums. Suutari (2002) concluded that empirical evidence was still weak in global leadership development programs and recommended more research on what is developed from programs such as an international assignment.

Caligiuri (2006) recommended more detailed research of developing global leaders. The development process is characterized by knowledge, skills and abilities, and personality characteristics. Caligiuri (2006) believed knowledge was possible to develop, skills and abilities were difficult to develop, and personality characteristics were very difficult to develop or change.

Based on the degree of difficulty in the developmental process, Caligiuri (2006) proposed interventions. The interventions for knowledge were areas such as reading books and doing e-learning courses. For skills and abilities, Caligiuri (2006) prescribed experiential intervention such as working on global teams, coaching, and mentoring. Intensive experience was recommended for personality characteristics. The intensive experience needed to be life-changing to help the global leader develop (Caligiuri, 2006).

Terrell and Rosenbusch (2013) claimed that global leadership development can help increase the speed of competence in the organization. Terrell and Rosenbusch concluded that global leaders develop and learn intuitively, dynamically employing ad hoc learning approaches. There were three factors that connected the learning approaches of global leaders. The first is attitude or stance toward learning. A second learning approach is utilizing ad hoc learning tactics. Third is utilizing reflection after experiences (Terrell & Rosenbusch, 2013).

Maak, Pless, and Borecka (2014) described the critical importance of developing responsible global leaders. To develop these competencies for responsible global leaders, a developmental program has to (a) trigger global mindset learning; (b) teach executives to deal with global social and environmental challenges; (c) improve the emotional and relational abilities of the global leaders to cope with relational challenges.

Maak, Pless, and Borecka (2014) researched multiple global leadership development programs and determined the importance of 360-degree feedback. In the 360-degree feedback, the global leader compares the self-assessment with the observation of his/her leadership by colleagues. The 360-degree feedback is one of the features of the International Service Learning Program (ISLP) that is used to increase the global leadership competencies of leaders.

From the review of research on learning and development and global leadership development, I make the following conclusions:

1. Anyone has the opportunity and ability to lead. The skillsets to be an effective leader can be learned. Leaders are not born as part of a certain few 'philosopher-kings'.
2. Although leadership can be learned, the type of leadership style and leadership behavior will differ according to context and

complexities. A village leader in Cambodia will have a different zone of development than a business leader of a multi-national organization in Dubai.

3. Leadership development is centered on learning. It is important to understand how each person learns in order to fully develop them as a leader. Leadership development is not mass-production training.

4. Goals and objectives must be set for each individual at the beginning. These goals have to be within the leader's zone of proximal development in order to be successful.

Below is an example of how I have approached this process in the Nextgen Global Leaders program. Here are a few ideas to illustrate my learning and development approach using the five principles. My focus is on organizational leaders, which is a different approach than individual leadership development.

Principle #1 Integrity

Power of reflective writing

Today, we see the lack of integrity of leaders around the world. This has affected the lives of companies and individuals greatly, and it has driven my passion to spread this principle to people around the world.

As the world economy is facing one of the hardest times in recent history, the lack of integrity in leadership is more prevalent than ever. Leadership is not graded when things are going smoothly and money is passed around in a bucket. Leadership is graded in times of crisis. It's when people look up and say, "Where is my help coming from?" The masses look for someone to follow who is admirable, trustworthy, honest, and authentic. How many leaders in the current financial crises can you describe as having these traits and characteristics?

We look at TVs, newspapers, and websites seeking these people, but the issue is not with the one leader but a group of leaders. The problems we are facing today in the world economy come from the lack of leadership throughout global companies not just by the one CEO or the handful in upper management. The more daunting fact is the only way we can successfully move through this time is with trained and empowered leaders. And if we are in this trouble because of lack of leadership, and the only way out is through effective leadership, we are in for a difficult ride!

As I lead a company, my integrity with my employees has been tested greatly. What do I sacrifice; what do my actions show? Do I lead with a self-seeking purpose, or do I lead as a servant leader. As thoughts of self-preservation and selfish success crowd my mind, I hear what was taught to me, "You lead to help others, not yourself."

There is evidence of large corporations understanding the practice of integrity and how it affects every part of the business. In the April 2007 Harvard Business Review, "Avoiding Integrity Land Mines," written by Ben W. Heineman, Jr., showed how GE understood the connection between leadership and integrity. Heineman was not an academic writing from the outside; he was GE's senior vice president and general counsel from 1987 to 2003, so his experience was the guide in the article:

Ultimately, it is a company's culture that sustains high performance with high integrity. Leaders and employees compete ferociously and meet tough economic goals lawfully and ethically not only because they are afraid of being caught and punished but because the company's norms and values are so widely shared and its reputation for integrity is so strong that most leaders and employees want to win the right way. (Heineman, 2007)

As a person develops into a leader, he or she has to establish a strict ethical code to live by. We call this integrity, and we hold strictly to this ethical code. Who wants to follow someone untrustworthy and irresponsible? This ethical code establishes the zone in which you operate as a leader.

Exercise

1. Write down when you are challenged with a moral zone.
2. Reflect in your writing the entire situation. Who is involved? What is the environment in which you are making the decision?
3. After making the decision, reflect on the outcomes of the decision. Did you play within your zone or break your ethical code?

Principle #2 Purpose/Vision

As I am roaring through my early forties, I understand this principle much better than when I was in my teens and twenties. On May 28, 2000, in Cairo, Egypt, I finally caught a clear glimpse of my purpose. It was life changing because for the first time, the focus was not about what I could achieve, but how I could best serve others.

My physical journey would take me through Egypt, Jordan, and back to the U.S. All of the travel and moving was to chase my purpose. Purpose as a principle of leadership is about others. Leadership is not a title but an action, the act of purpose is an important principle in establishing yourself as a leader.

Below is a list of questions to assess your purpose and help you define your purpose as a leader.

Purpose Assessment

1. Describe your purpose.
2. What efforts have you made to work toward the purpose?
3. Have you attracted others to follow the purpose?
4. What skills do you need to be more effective leading others with a shared purpose?

Principle #3 Sacrifice

Developing Humble Organizational Leaders

In creating a leadership developmental program, there are many complex issues of evaluation and assessment of context (Hamilton & Bean, 2005). Understanding propositional knowledge is a much-debated topic. "Our beliefs often gain their justification via inference, and inference is a phenomenon of understanding - of seeing connections between conclusion and premises" (Roberts &Wood, 2007, p.48). So how does one gain propositional knowledge such as humility? It is more than just believing that humility is good; a person has to gain an understanding of the virtue. The understanding builds the foundation for propositional knowledge to grow (Roberts &Wood, 2007). To gain understanding takes a will and a desire to build upon knowledge. A person cannot be coerced into learning humility.

If humility is a skill to be learned, then the next question is how to develop a method for teaching organizational leaders to be humble. Evidence shows that learning propositional knowledge is better in a group setting. For leadership and development, there are many options.

Developing Humility in Organizational Leaders

To accomplish the task of developing the emerging leadership theory into a leadership development program, it is important to survey similar approaches. In the past, the words *authentic* and *servant* described the humble leader. Because authentic and servant leadership theories have a virtue-based, ethical foundation, they provide an opportunity to compare the implementation of the programs. I extract leadership development from other theories to build a framework for humility development in organizations. The leadership development program frames, measures, and sustains humility in organizations.

Framing

An essential element of leadership development programs is framing (Hamilton & Bean, 2005). "As a social process, framing influences meaning by focusing attention on some cues while masking others" (Hamilton & Bean, 2005, p. 338). Meaning-making is one element of framing. Because of various contexts of word utilizations, a consistent language is required to effectively develop leaders in humility. "Language evokes values, and along with selecting cues from the environment, it is essential in framing" (Hamilton & Bean, 2005, p. 338).

Another element of framing is sensemaking. Through individual and social activities, leaders can learn in an organizational context (Hamilton & Bean, 2005). The context of the social activities does vary according to cultures. Another culture will have a different value and belief, which causes framing to loose effectiveness in training (Hamilton & Bean, 2005). The inability to frame the appropriate definition of an important word or concept could derail the success of the program. An example of this problem occurred when a company from the southeastern part of the United States expanded into the United Kingdom. The company struggled to frame the same meaning of servant leadership from American English to British English, which caused the program to flutter and lose the ability to develop the leaders (Hamilton & Bean, 2005).

Question:

1. How do you frame humility in your organization? Is it viewed in your organization as courageous or weak?

Measurement

In order to measure humility development, there needs to be a clear definition to construct the framework needed for measurement (Cooper, Scandura, & Schriesheim, 2005). Once a clear definition is established, then "it will be necessary to use pretest-posttest study designs and difference measures to reduce the inflation of training effect estimates due to pretest-training interactions" (Cooper, Scandura, & Schriesheim, 2005, p.479). Along with surveys, a tool needs to provide interaction with participants to provide data on decision-making especially concerning ethics and virtues (Cooper, Scandura, & Schriesheim, 2005).

Humility development's ability to succeed also hinges on the issue of distinguishing itself from other measurement tools, such as the Multifactor Leadership Questionnaire (MLQ) for transformational leadership (Cooper, Scandura, & Schriesheim, 2005). To distinguish the theory is to provide a root construct that differs from other leadership theories such as transformational, servant, and charismatic leadership. Cooper, Scandura, and Schriesheim (2005) note that until there is empirical evidence that discriminates this theory from other theories, it is not possible to start the process of measurement and development.

In contrast to authentic leadership development, servant leadership development does have case studies that provide the constructs for measurement (Sendjaya, Sarros, & Santora, 2008). Below is an illustration of the construct that is used to categorize qualitative studies on servant leadership development.

The important factor to note in measuring servant leadership is that there are existing models to utilize. These models do have validation, and by integrating them with other leadership modals, an extensive qualitative data research can be accomplished (Sendjaya et al., 2008). Servant leadership also has a content validity ratio (CVR). CVR=(nΣ-N/2)/N/2. N is the total number of experts surveyed and nΣ is the experts who listed the developmental trait as essential.

Question:

1. What acts of humility can you measure in your organization?

Principle #4 Discipline

My application of discipline was developed after almost dropping out of college. As I found myself between semesters submitting an application to the textile mill that my grandparents and parents worked so hard in to prevent me from having to work there, I saw that my lack of discipline was the main reason for my lack of success in college. So I moved to Birmingham and thought that working full-time and finishing my undergrad at night and weekends was the answer. It turned out to be the right decision at the time. The discipline I learned during that stage in my life became the foundation when I founded and led Sun Consulting Services, LLC. On a daily basis, I managed multiple offices in the U.S. and Asia. We had partners I collaborated with in the Middle East, Africa and Europe.

Of course, I had my challenges in following through with the application. One of my challenges in managing my time and setting priorities is that I like to be around other people. I am energized by being around other people like a typical extravert and this causes problems with time efficiency. To set aside large chunks of time for work and strategic planning means I have to say no to being around people. This is hard for me.

Another challenge in achieving this principle of discipline is my short attention span. I have never been able to concentrate on something for a long period of time. My mind is always running with ideas or thoughts that usually distract my attention from a priority. I was in graduate school before I mastered the ability to force myself to read more than 10 minutes at a time. I am purely a visual person, and this is why I love the invention of video podcast. Now I can watch people talk which is much more engaging.

In overcoming these challenges, it is important for the leader to learn self-control. You have to develop a pattern of discipline that allows for you to continue learning and expanding your capabilities. Years ago, I listened to Zig Zigler on a podcast. He was over 70 years old and still learning how to become a better leader. He disciplined himself to read over 3 hours per day to sharpen his mind and be able to deliver effective concepts for motivation.

In developing as a leader, the principle of discipline is one of the most difficult, and you never completely master it. You regularly need to find a way to properly assess your discipline in the areas of time and priority management on a regular basis.

Where does the time go?

Record how you used each hour of your time for the last two working days during regular business hours. For each block of time, describe what you were doing, and write if it was productive or a time waster?

Questions:

1. In what areas do you invest your time wisely?
2. What are your time wasters?
3. What do you need to change in your daily routine?

Principle #5 Compassion

One of the great leaders in the Bible is Moses. He constantly demonstrated the leadership principle of compassion as he led the Israelites out of Egypt. Many times he had to defend Israel before God in order for them not to be severely punished for their actions. On one occasion in Exodus 32:10-12 (New International Version) it says,

10 Now leave me (God) alone so that my anger may burn against them and that I may destroy them. Then I will make you into a great nation." 11 But Moses sought the favor of the LORD his God. "O LORD," he said, "why should your anger burn against your people, whom you brought out of Egypt with great power and a mighty hand? 12 Why should the Egyptians say, 'It was with evil intent that he brought them out, to kill them in the mountains and to wipe them off the face of the earth'? Turn from your fierce anger; relent and do not bring disaster on your people.

As a leader, you are always forced to defend people to another authority. We are not like Moses, defending people to the Ultimate Authority, but we do have to show compassion for our followers and defend them to our bosses, clients, and investors. It is in this type of compassion that I have to grow. I still think primarily about myself when making decisions, and I do not always think through who is being affected. A leader sees the ripple effects of a decision and works through the decision with compassion.

I am convinced that the most effective leaders are those who have the most compassionate hearts. Since leadership is centered on serving followers, then the leaders that make a generational impact have actions full of compassion, humility, and care. As you think about your own journey of following leaders, how often did you follow a coercive, arrogant, and selfish leader?

Reflect about the leaders who have influenced your life the most, the ones whose leadership in your life constantly comes to mind. I am sure you can point to a time and place when you saw the principle of compassion in them. Maybe it was a football coach who brought you home from practice and took time to listen to your family problems or a student mentor who played basketball with you and discussed issues that challenged your beliefs and values. It could have been a teacher who worked hard to help you reach a goal or a business leader who took time to mentor you during the hard times of starting your company. All of these examples are of leaders who understand the leadership principle of compassion.

In the end, a compassionate leader will be an impactful leader who will provide a way to give hope to the hopeless, a hug to the hurting, a helping hand to the needy, and their heart to their followers. The challenge is how do you measure this on the compassion scale? Below is a quiz to help you understand your performance on the leadership principle of compassion. I am sure you will be able to properly assess if you pass the test at the end.

Leaders are Compassionate Quiz:

1. When making decisions do you think about yourself first or others?
2. How often each week do you show you care about someone without being asked to do something for them?
3. In measuring your time with others, how much do you listen instead of talk?
4. When is the last time you visited a coworker, friend, or family member in the hospital?
5. When was the last time you served someone?

9

GOING FORWARD

Our current culture wants everything instantly. We want fast Internet at home, on our phone, and even on the plane. Everything seems to move at a fast pace as we go about our day-to-day lives. The problem for global leaders is that although one of the complexities is rate of change in the world, the process of leadership development is still slow. There is not a fast-track system to learning how to manage the complexities of global leadership. Learning to be a leader is a lifelong journey.

My goal in writing my book is to serve you. I hope I have accomplished this by helping you understand what a global leader is:

> A *Global leader is a person who leads across cultures to perform complex leadership with systems, processes, and relationships.*

What is complexity and why is global leadership more complex than domestic leadership? Complexity is the ability to survive and thrive in situations of limited information. The global leader usually makes decisions with limited information, and for that reason the cognitive complexity of global leadership increases compared to complexities of domestic leadership. Although there is an increase of empirical research in global leadership, it is still far behind empirical studies in domestic leadership because many academics still contemplate the presence of differences in competencies for a global leader vs. a traditional domestic leader. In other words, many academics see global leadership as one of the many theories of leadership. This is not how I frame global leadership. Global leadership should have its own field of study separate from domestic leadership studies because global leadership isn't just one type of leadership style. It is separate from theories like transformational and servant leadership.

Finally, I described five leadership principles that from my experience allow global leaders to manage the complexities in systems, processes, and relationships. These five are the foundational principles that all leaders need to exhibit in their lives.

The Five Leadership Principles

Principle #1 Integrity

Adheres to and acts in alignment with a set of core values and beliefs; keeps his/ her word and commitments; establishes credibility with others by 'walking the talk; provides honest feedback in an appropriate and helpful manner; admits mistakes; doesn't misrepresent self for personal gain; maintains confidentiality; is seen as a truthful and trustworthy leader.

In global leadership, your character is tested on a regular basis. Each crisis of leadership will require a global leader to decipher core values from cultural values. Before one can decipher these differences, one must have a clear understanding of personal core values.

Principle #2 Purpose

Understands and clearly articulates an inspired vision of the company's goals and mission; aligns team's goals with company's goals; committed to the company's core values and culture.

The articulation depends not just on the words used but on character and integrity. When leading across cultures, the global leader must carefully communicate the vision in order to ensure it is effective in reaching the target audience.

Principle #3 Sacrifice

A leader is willing to sacrifice in three primary areas.

1. *Individual- Being a leader means you sacrifice individually in order for your purpose to be achieved.*
2. *Family- In leadership you constantly have to ask your family to sacrifice, and that is why they have to believe in your cause just as much as you do.*
3. *Those you serve- As a leader it seems that everyone wants a piece of your attention and time. Even the people you serve will need to sacrifice and allow you to grow as a leader.*

The demands of travel alone are enough to challenge the sacrificial ability of a global leader and his family. But an even greater challenge for a global leader is sacrificing one's local identity in order to gain global followers.

Principle #4 Discipline

Discipline is an aspect of self-control. A leader has to be disciplined in many areas, but the two most important are time and priorities. The leader who is disciplined with time and priorities accomplishes goals and objectives.

Virtual teams and time zone differences are some of the challenges that require the global leader to manage time and priorities well. The ability to lead change also takes a discipline that is unique.

Principle #5 Compassion

Compassion is extremely important in becoming a leader and most of all in developing new leaders for the next generation. Of all the soft skills, this is the most extreme soft skill, but a leader struggles without it because the essence of leadership is having loyal followers and being able to develop more leaders. Without the leadership principle of compassion, a leader will struggle to develop others into effective leaders.

Compassion is a hard trait to exhibit in one's own culture and even more so in multiple cultures. How a global leader communicates to and treats the next generation of leaders is as important as the process. A wrong word or cultural insensitivity can cause a leader to be labeled as weak or hegemonistic. Either description is damaging to relationships and decreases the effectiveness of leadership.

Of all the leadership principles, these five are the building blocks for other characteristics of an effective leader. We all have an opportunity to lead in some part of life, but the leaders who implement these principles will leave a positive legacy. If leaders follow these principles in their lives and practices, they will see fruit from the investment. They will build credibility and experiences that will attract followers. And you are not a leader unless you have followers.

I am not an exception to this rule. Even with all my experiences that I've detailed in this book, I still have a long way to go in my journey as a global leader. My hope is that this book will help you identify areas where you need to develop as a global leader, and it will start a fascinating journey of growth for you and your purpose.

Bibliography

Adler, N. J., & Bartholomew, S. (1992). Managing globally competent people. Executive, 6, 52-65. doi:10.5465/AME.1992.4274189.

Anderson, D. L. (2012). *Organizational development: The process of leading organizational change.* Thousand Oaks, CA: Sage.

Bass, B., Avolio, B. (Ed.). (1994). *Improving organizational effectiveness: Through sacrificial leadership.* Thousand Oaks, CA. Sage Publishing.

Bird, A. (2013). Mapping the content domain of global leadership competencies. In Mendenhall, M.E., Osland, J.S., Bird, A, Oddou, G.R., Maznevski, M.L., Stevens, M.J., & Stahl, G.K. (Eds.), *Global leadership: research, practice, and development* (pp. 80-96). New York: Routledge.

Blanchard, K. (2007). *Leading at a higher level.* Upper Saddle River, NJ: Pearson.

Burke, W. (2011). *Organization change: Theory and practice 3rd edition.* Los Angeles, CA: Sage.

Burke, Warner W., Lake, Dale G. and Paine, Jill W. (eds.) (2009). *Organization Change, A Comprehensive Reader.* Wiley.

Burns, J. M. (1978). *Leadership.* New York, NY: HarperCollins.

Burtis, J., & Turman, P. (2010). *Leadership communication as citizenship.* Los Angeles, CA: Sage.

Caligiuri, P. M. (2006). Developing global leaders. *Human Resource Management Review*, 16: 219–228.

Caligiuri, P., & Tarique, I. (2009). Predicting effectiveness in global leadership activities. *Journal of World Business, 44: 336–346.*

Caligiuri, P., & Tarique, I. (2012). Dynamic cross-cultural competencies and global leadership effectiveness. *Journal of World Business, 47*, 612-622.

Cambodian Development Review Institute. (2010). *Cambodian Development Review, April-June 2010.* [Data File and Code Book]. Retrieved from http://www.cdri.org.kh

Carbonell, M., Ponz, S. R. (2006). *Uniquely you personalizing my faith: Membership and ministry profile.* Blue Ridge, GA: Uniquely You. Collins, J. (2009). *How the mighty fall.* London, UK: Random House.

Conner, Daryl R. (2006) *Managing at the speed of change.* New York, NY, Random House. Anderson, D. L. (2012). *Organizational development: The process of leading organizational change.* Thousand Oaks, CA: Sage.

Cooper, C. D., Scandura, T. A., & Schriesheim, C. A. (2005). Looking forward but learning from our past: Potential challenges to developing authentic leadership theory and authentic leaders. *The Leadership Quarterly, 16*(3), 475-493. doi: 10.1016/j.leaqua.2005.03.008

Cloud, H. *(2006). Integrity : the courage to meet the demands of reality. New York: Collins.*

Crossan, M., Vera, D., & Nanjad, L. (2008). Transcendent leadership: Strategic leadership in dynamic environments. *The Leadership Quarterly, 19*(5), 569-581. doi: 10.1016/j.leaqua.2008.07.008

Crutchfield, L.R. & McLeod Grant, H. (2008) *Forces for good: The six practices of high-impact social entrepreneurs*. San Francisco, CA: Josey-Bass.

Dent, E. (2013). The Design, Development, and Evaluation of Measures to Survey Worldview in Organizations (September 17, 2013). Available at SSRN: http://ssrn.com/abstract=2326908 or http://dx.doi.org/10.2139/ssrn.2326908

Dragoni, L. & McAlpine, K. (2012). Leading the business: The criticality of global leaders' cognitive complexity in setting strategic directions. *Industrial and Organizational Psychology, 5 (2)*, 237-240.

Drucker, P. (1986). *The practice of management*. New York, NY: HarperCollins.

Drucker, P. (1990). *Managing the social entrepreneurs organization*. New York, NY: HarperCollins.

Drucker, P. F. (2003). *The essential Ducker: The best of sixty years of Peter Drucker's essential writings on management*. New York: HarperBusiness.

Fiedler, F.E. (1971). Validation and extension of the contingency model of leadership effectiveness: A review of empirical findings. *Psychological Bulletin, 76*, 128-148.

Food and Agriculture Organization of the United Nations. (2010). *FAO Statistics Yearbook*. [Data File and Code Book]. Retrieved from http://www.fao.org/ economic/ess/ess-publications/ess-yearbook/ess-yearbook2010/yearbook2010-welfare/en/

Furtner, M. R., Rauthmann, J. F., & Sachse, P. (2010). The Socioemotionally Intelligent self-leader: Examining relations between self-leadership and socioemotional intelligence. *Social Behavior & Personality: An International Journal, 38*(9), 1191-1196. doi: 10.2224/sbp.2010.38.9.1191.

Gersick, C.J. (1991). Revolutionary change theories: A multilevel exploration of the punctuated equilibrium paradigm. *Academy of Management Review, 16 (1),* 10-36.

Gitsham, M. (2008) "Developing the global leader of tomorrow." Conference presentation at the 1ˢᵗ Global Forum for Responsible Management Education, United Nations, New York, December 4-5, 2008.

Goethals, G. R., Sorenson, G. L. (Ed.). (2007). *The quest for a general theory of leadership.* Northampton, MA: Edward Elgar.

Gold, J., Thorpe, R., Mumford, A. (Ed.). (2010). *Handbook of leadership and management development.* Retrieved from http://books.google.com/books

Goleman, D., Boyatzis, R. E., & McKee, A. (2002). *Primal leadership: realizing the power of emotional intelligence.* Boston, Mass.: Harvard Business School Press.

Greenleaf, R. K. (2002). *Servant leadership: A journey into the nature of legitimate power and greatness.* Mahwah, NJ: Paulist Press.

Gregersen, H. B., Morrison, A. J., & Black, J. S. (1998). Developing leaders for the global frontier. *Sloan Management Review, 40*(1): 21–32.

Hamilton, F., & Bean, C. J. (2005). The importance of context, beliefs and values in leadership development. *Business Ethics: A European Review, 14*(4), 336-347. doi: 10.1111/j.1467-8608.2005.00415.x

Hayes, M., & Comer, M. (2011). Lead with humility. *Leadership Excellence, 28*(9), 13-13.

Heifetz, R. A. (1994). *Leadership without easy answers.* Cambridge, Mass.: Belknap Press of Harvard University Press.

Heineman, B. W. (2007). Avoiding integrity land mines. *Harvard business review, 85*(4), 100.

Hofstede, G. (1980). Motivation, leadership and organization: Do american theories apply abroad? *Organizational Dynamics. Summer 1980.* 42-63.

Holt, K. & Seki, K. (2012). Global leadership: A developmental shift for everyone. *Industrial and Organizational Psychology. 5 (2).* 196-215.

Jackson, T. (2009). A critical cross-cultural perspective for developing nonprofit international management capacity. Nonprofit Management & Leadership. 19 (4). 443-466.

Johnson, C. (2009). *Meeting the ethical challenges of leadership: Casting light or shadow* (3rd ed.). Thousand Oaks, CA: Sage.

Jokinen, T. (2005). Global leadership competencies: a review and discussion. *Journal of European Industrial Training, 29 (3)*; 199-216.

Kant, I. (1952). *Kant.* Chicago, IL: Encyclopedia Brittannica, Inc.

King, Jr., M.L. (2003). *I Have a Dream: Writings and Speeches That Changed the World.* San Francisco, CA: HarperOne

Kouzes, J., & Posner, B. (2012). *The leadership challenge.* (5th ed.). San Francisco, CA: Jossey-Bass.

Louden, R. B. (2007). Kantian moral humility: Between Aristotle and Paul. *Philosophy & Phenomenological Research, 75*(3), 632-639. doi: 10.1111/j.1933-1592.2007.00098.x

Luban, D. (2006). Making sense of moral meltdowns. In Rhode, D. (Ed.), *Moral leadership: The theory and practice of power, judgment, and policy (pp. 57-76).* San Francisco, CA: Jossey-Bass.

Margolis, J. & Molinsky A. (2006). Three practical challenges of moral leadership. In Rhode, D. (Ed.), *Moral leadership: The theory and practice of power, judgment, and policy (pp. 77-94).* San Francisco, CA: Jossey-Bass.

Maak, T., Pless, N., & Borecka, M. (2014). Developing responsible global leaders. In Osland, J., Li, M., & Wang, Y. (Eds.). *Advances in global leadership. (Vol 8, pp.339-364).* Bingley, U.K.: Emerald Group Publishing.

Machiavelli, N. (1515) *The prince.* (W.K. Marriott, Trans.), Paperview U.K. Ltd. (n.d.)

McCall, M. W., Jr., & Hollenbeck, G. P. (2002). *Developing global executives: The lessons of international experience.* Boston, MA: Harvard Business School Press.

Mendenhall, M., Reiche, B., Bird, A., & Osland, J. (2012). Defining the "global" in global leadership. *Journal of World Business, 47,* 493-503.

Moore, C. & Tenbrunsel, A. (2014). "Just think about it?" Cognitive complexity and moral choice. *Organizational Behavior and Human Decision Processes,* 123, 138-149.

Morgan, G. (2006). *Images of organizations.* Thousand Oaks, CA: Sage.

Morris, J. A., Brotheridge, C. M., & Urbanski, J. C. (2005). Bringing humility to leadership: Antecedents and consequences of leader humility. *Human Relations, 58*(10), 1323-1350. doi: 10.1177/0018726705059929

Morrison, A. & Black, J. (2014). The character of global leaders. In Osland, J., Li, M., & Wang, Y. (Eds.). *Advances in global leadership. (Vol 8, pp.183-204).* Bingley, U.K.: Emerald Group Publishing.

Neck, C., & Manz, C. (2013). *Mastering self-leadership: Empowering yourself for personal excellence* (6th ed.). Boston, MA: Pearson.

Northouse, P. G. (2010). *Leadership: Theory and Practice* (Fifth ed.). Los Angeles, CA: SAGE.

Park, N., Peterson, C., & Seligman, M. P. (2004). Strengths of character and well-being. *Journal of Social & Clinical Psychology, 23*(5), 603-619.

Patterson, K., Dannhauser, Z., & Stone, A.G. (2007). From noble to global: The attributes of global leadership. Servant Leadership Research Roundtable Proceedings. Regent.

Patterson, S., & Radtke, J. (2009). *Strategic communications for nonprofit organizations: Seven steps to creating a successful plan.* Hoboken, NJ: John Wiley & Sons.

Petrick, J. A., Scherer, R. F., Brodzinski, J. D., Quinn, J. F., & Ainina, M. F. (1999). Global leadership skills and reputational capital: Intangible resources for sustainable competitive advantage. *Academy of Management Executive, 13*(1): 58–69.

Rhode, D. (Ed.). (2006). *Moral leadership: The theory and practice of power, judgment, and policy.* San Francisco, CA: Jossey-Bass.

Riggio, R. E., Murphy, S. E., & Pirozzolo, F. J. (2001). *Multiple intelligences and leadership.* Lawrence Erlbaum Associates, Inc. Retrieved from EBSCO*host.*

Roberts, R., & Wood, W., (2007). *Intellectual virtues: An essay in regulative epistemology.* Oxford, UK: Oxford University Press.

Runde, C., & Flanagan, T. (2013). *Becoming a conflict competent leader: How you and your organization can manage conflict effectively.* San Francisco, CA: Jossey-Bass.

Rus, D., Van Knippenberg, D., & Wisse, B. (2012). Leader power and self-serving behavior: The moderating role of accountability. *The Leadership Quarterly, 23*(1), 13-26.

Schein, E. H. (2011). Humble Inquiry. *Leadership Excellence, 28*(4), 4-4.

Sendjaya, S., Sarros, J. C., & Santora, J. C. (2008). Defining and measuring servant leadership behaviour in organizations. *Journal of Management Studies, 45*(2), 402-424. doi: 10.1111/j.1467-6486.2007.00761.x

Sidle, C. (2007). The five intelligences of leadership. *Leader to Leader*, 43, 19- 25. Retrieved from EBSCO*host*.

Smith, W.& Lewis, M. (2011). Toward a theory of paradox: A dynamic equilibrium model of organizing. *Academy of Management Review. 36 (2).* 381-403

Solomon, R. (1999). *A better way to think about business: How personal integrity leads to corporate success.* New York, NY: Oxford Press.

Spreitzer, G. M., McCall, M. W., Jr., & Mahoney, J. (1997). Global leadership skills and reputational capital: Intangible resources for sustainable competitive advantage. *Journal of Applied Psychology, 82(*1): 6–29.

Stodgill, R. (1948). Personal factors associated with leadership: A survey of the literature. *The Journal of Psychology, 25 (1),* 35-71.

Sternberg, Robert. (1999). The theory of successful intelligence. *Review of General Psychology,* 3(4), 292-316.

Suutari, V. (2002). Global leader development: An emerging research agenda. *Career Development International, 7(*4): 218–233.

Terrell, S., & Rosenbusch, K. (2013). Global leadership development: What global organizations can do to reduce leadership risk, increase speed of competence, and build global leadership muscle. *People and Strategy, 36* (1), 40-46.

The National Center for Charitable Statistics. (2011). *IRS Business Master Files.* [Data File and Code Book] Retrieved from<u>http://nccs.urban.org/ statistics/quickfacts.cfm</u>

Tubbs, S. & Schulz, E. (2006). Exploring a taxonomy of global leadership competencies and meta-competencies. *The Journal of American Academy of Business. 8 (2).* 29-34.

United Nations, Department of Economic and Social Affairs. (2011). *World Population Prospects.* [Data File and Code Book]. Retrieved from http://esa.un.org/unpd/ wpp/index.htm.

UNICEF (2014)Http:// http://www.unicefusa.org/mission/survival/water

Vera, D., & Rodriguez-Lopez, A. (2004). Strategic Virtues: Humility as a Source of Competitive Advantage. [Article]. *Organizational Dynamics, 33*(4), 393-408. doi: 10.1016/j.orgdyn.2004.09.006

Vygotski, L. S. (1978). *Mind in society the development of higher psychological processes.* Cambridge, Mass.; London: Harvard University Press.

Vygotski, L. S. (1986). *Thought and language.* A. Kozulin, (Ed.). Cambridge, MA: The MIT Press.

Weick, K.E. (2009). *Making sense of the organization: The impermananet organization.* West Sussex, U.K: Wiley and Sons.

Weisberg, J. (2010). "Evolutionary" and "revolutionary" events affecting HRM in Israel: 1948-2008. *Human Resource Managment Review, 20,* 176-185.

Wills, S. & Barham, K. (1992). Being an international manager. *European Management Journal, 12 (1)*; 49-58.

Yukl, G. (2008). How leaders influence organizational effectiveness. *Leadership Quarterly, 19*(6), 708-722.

Yukl, G. (2010). *Leadership in organizations* (7th ed.). Upper Saddle River, NJ: Prentice Hall.

Yunnis, M. (2007). *Creating a world without poverty: Social business and the future of capitalism.* New York, NY: BBS Public Affairs

Zaccaro, S. (2007). Trait-based perspectives of leadership. *American Psychologist, 62(1),* 6-16.

—

Author Bio

B. Jay Clark, Ph.D.

B. Jay Clark currently lives in Texas in the Dallas/Ft. Worth area. Jay and his wife Anne have five daughters. Jay's background is comprised of starting companies and non-profit organizations. He has both academic and practical experience in developing global leaders in the for-profit and non-profit sectors.

From over 15 years of consulting experience in the United States and in international markets, Jay has gained valuable insights on strategy development, management challenges and practices, and leadership development. Jay founded Sun Consulting Services and managed the offices in the U.S. and Hong Kong. Under Jay's leadership, Sun Consulting was a pioneer in China for the consulting industry by working with a state-owned oil/gas company and a large publicly traded technology company. Jay has developed a network of global partners in Asia, Africa, Europe, India, and the Middle East for Sun Consulting Services.

From his experiences of living in five countries on four different continents and working in emerging markets, Jay developed the Nextgen Global Leaders Program. This program is for corporations and non-profit organizations that are transforming into global companies and need to identify, train, and manage top talent in order to expand globally. Jay has worked with HR departments of both large and small organizations to link their corporate strategy with the leadership development program. Jay specializes in helping firms increase profits with global strategies that include Market Assessments, Market Entry, Global Channel/Distribution Management, Sourcing Products, and Investments.

Jay received his Ph.D. in Leadership Studies from Tennessee Temple University. He earned an MBA from Auburn University with a concentration in leadership, and during his graduate training, he studied at the Czech Management Center in Prague, Czech Republic. His research was on companies doing business in emerging markets. Jay received his B.S. in Management from the University of Alabama at Birmingham.

Made in the USA
Middletown, DE
22 July 2021